Date Due

	NOV 14		
MAY 18			
MAR 5	MAR 27 1996		
OCT 14			
OCT 30			
MAY 24			
MAR 24			
APR 8			
JAN 8			
MAR 9			
APR 15			
MAR 3			
DEC 17			
JAN 26			
NOV 24			
OCT 13			
NOV 8			
APR 5	PRINTED	IN U. S. A.	

WILL ROGERS

"Everybody liked him, and he liked everybody." That was Will Rogers, homespun philosopher, comedian, and motion-picture star.

WILL ROGERS

Ambassador of Good Will
Prince of Wit and Wisdom

By

P. J. O'BRIEN

NAVY AVIATION SERVICE, WORLD WAR

WITH AN APPRECIATION

By

LOWELL THOMAS

Illustrated

THE JOHN C. WINSTON COMPANY

CHICAGO   PHILADELPHIA   TORONTO

WILL ROGERS

THE CHARACTER and temperament of an age as well as its common sense are reflected in its laughter." So says Dr. J. C. Gregory in his treatise on the *Sense of Humor*. He remarks further: "The way men laugh and the things they laugh at reflect their tastes, thoughts, and sympathies. . . . Society offers its pulse in the nature of its laughter."

The career of Will Rogers is the finest illustration you could find of these observations. If we hadn't had him during the last ten years, if we hadn't appreciated him and had the sense to laugh with him and at ourselves, we should have been a sad people.

He first burgeoned out as the Smiling Prophet of America in the era of the Great Insanity, the period we remember because of the tragic comedy of Teapot Dome, which culminated in the cataclysm of November, 1929. Political magnificos worried and denounced; editors exploded in 12-point type. Rogers poured out a steady stream of sparkling common sense that helped us to maintain some sort of perspective.

When the Depression descended upon us in such volume that not even the most ostrich-minded could deny it, the man from Oklahoma stuck out among us as a flashing tower of sanity. And people listened to him.   Historians and economists tried to remind us that there had been previous depressions and that the Republic had survived.   But we needed the droll, jovial gags of Will Rogers to make us keep our feet on the ground.

One of the finest facts about him was that he never took a crack at any man—either a man, a party, or a class—unless he or it was riding cockily on top of the world.   For example: his most ludicrous comment upon bankers was delivered at a time when they were the Sacred White Cows of every editorial office in America.   It was in 1924 that Rogers came out with the paragraph: "Vanderlip made a speech at the Rotary Club of Ossining, New York, that astonished the United States. . . . Rotary is composed of one of the best of each line of work or business. . . . Mr. Vanderlip must have felt right at home up there.   There are more bankers at Ossining than any town of its size in the United States."

If that had been said in 1933, it would have been an obvious, almost cowardly jab.   But at the time that Rogers published it, bankers were still the High Priests of Finance, quoted with reverence upon any subject from world politics to birth control.

After the pendulum had swung, after they had become a general target for abuse, Rogers declined to join the chorus.   Instead, he turned the fire of his comedic machine guns upon the people who were kicking the bankers.   As he said himself with his unforgettable grin: "I'm always agin' the party that's up."   At the height of the Teapot Dome

Scandal, he kidded Senator Walsh, the prosecutor, as merrily as he did Sinclair and Doheny. Later on, when the bankers were in the pillory, Rogers aimed his most pointed barbs at their inquisitors, Senator Black and Counselor Ferdie Pecora. On all such occasions, the essence of his quality was that he made everybody like it. Some of us winced a bit, but after we had caught our breath, we all had to join in the laughter.

Since his death the pundits have been saying that Rogers had not as deep a background of philosophy as Mark Twain. How Will would have chuckled at the suggestion. But if you consider his jesting as a whole, you will see that the gum-chewing master of the lariat had one of the soundest and oldest of all philosophies in the world—a fine scorn for all shams and pretensions. It was always the bumptious, the poseurs, at whom he poked the most fun. He had an amazing faculty for penetrating poses, equaled only by his ability to do it without venom.

One of the principal differences between him and Mark Twain was that Rogers lacked capacity for the fierce indignation to which Clemens gave vent in his later years.

In describing *Innocents Abroad*, Stephen Leacock has aptly observed that "Mark Twain could see Europe more clearly from the top of the Rockies than could the people walking in the Rue de Rivoli or sitting around the Forum in Rome." Rogers had a good measure of the same faculty. He could see not only Europe but his own country. But it never made him indignant.

The only pose in Will Rogers was the pretense that he was an ignorant and illiterate fellow. Actually he was nothing of the sort. As he once remarked, "We are all of us ignorant, but not about the same things." Though he made a bluff at concealing it, his writings from time to time betrayed an exceedingly wide knowledge. Whether he was conscious of it or not, the system behind his humor was an exceedingly old one. It can be described in one word—Truth. It is one of the most ancient formulæ of the Comic Spirit. As Max Eastman has remarked: "Truth is a chief source of the joy motive in popular jokes. . . . We are always hungry for the simple truth."

That, in the last analysis, is what Will Rogers gave us.

Lowell Thomas

CONTENTS

CONTENTS

ACKNOWLEDGMENTS

The author's and publishers' sincere thanks are extended to V. V. McNitt, head of the McNaught Syndicate, who discovered the great ability of Will Rogers as a writer, for his permission to use portions of Rogers writings in this book. The author is deeply indebted to Friar Joe Laurie, Jr., for the use of hitherto little known material on Rogers from Laurie's own files; to Friar Vic Guinness for his unselfish interest and help; and to Mark Wilson of the Shubert organization for his worth-while assistance.

CHAPTER I

TRAGEDY OF THE TUNDRA

IN THE weird, half light of a summer night in the far Northland, a red, low-winged monoplane skimmed gracefully along the surface of a shallow river that pierced the bleak Alaskan tundra. The ship gained speed, climbed a scanty fifty feet, and then plunged awkwardly, out of control, to the water below. It was as if some invisible hunter with a powerful, silent weapon had sent a lethal charge into the gaily-colored, man-made bird. No one moved in the broken airplane. Its occupants had made their final landing.

Thus did Will Rogers, beloved prince of wit and wisdom, and Wiley Post, master aviator, meet their end in the barren wilderness a few miles from the last outpost of civilization in North America.

Only a terrified Eskimo seal hunter saw the ship as it crashed into the edge of the little unnamed stream, and in his fright he ran away from the tangled wreckage of the once-roaring machine of his white-faced brothers. As the echo of the crash rolled away over the hummocky tundra, the native, Clair Oakpeha, made his way back to the river bank and shouted loudly to the men in the plane. There was no answer. Only the Arctic stillness.

Realizing that the occupants of the plane were beyond his aid, Oakpeha set out to bring the news of the disaster to Point Barrow, fifteen miles away, northernmost point on the continent, where the United States Army Signal Corps maintains a radio station. Over the dry hummocks, through little streams wending their way into the Arctic Ocean and around tiny lakes, where nested the white, whistling swans and the black-necked geese, the Eskimo walked and raced until three hours later he reached the settlement. Exhausted, he stopped near the radio shack to gasp out to a group of natives: "Bird men dead. Red bird blow up."

Staff Sergeant Stanley R. Morgan, of the Signal Corps, the only representative of the Government north of Latitude 71°, heard the native's story, and from his pidgin English the soldier knew that the plane was that of Post and that the passenger was Will Rogers.

Out into the Arctic night went Sergeant Morgan to round up a crew of Eskimo seal hunters to go to the scene. In a whaleboat kicked along by an outboard motor, they churned their way south-ward through the little streams and across the tiny ponds. It was several hours later before they came upon the wreckage. The plane lay on its back in two feet of water, its right wing was crumpled, its engine jammed back into the cockpit.

HIS DAUGHTER'S PICTURE

In Rogers' pocket was his Ingersoll watch, still ticking, showing the time at 3.30 A. M. On Post's wrist was a smashed watch showing the time at 8.18 P. M.—the time of the crash on August 15,

Photo from Wide World Photos, Inc.

Mr. and Mrs. Rogers as they arrived in New York aboard the Ile de France after a trip around the world.

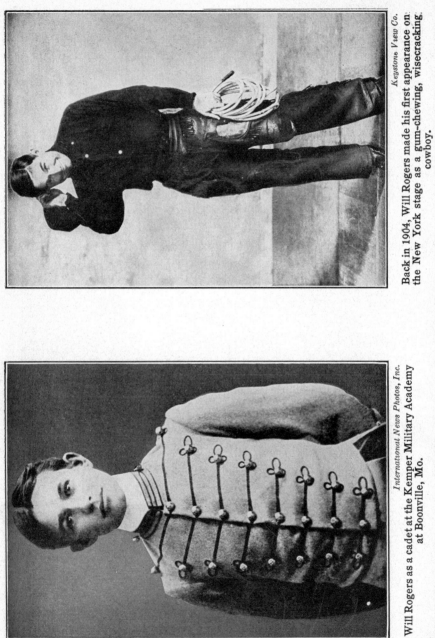

Will Rogers as a cadet at the Kemper Military Academy at Boonville, Mo.

Back in 1904, Will Rogers made his first appearance on the New York stage as a gum-chewing, wisecracking, cowboy.

1935. Both bodies were wrapped in blankets and placed in an *oomiak,* an Eskimo open boat made of skins stretched over a frame, and towed to Point Barrow. From Rogers' coat pocket fell a newspaper clipping bearing the picture of his eighteen-year-old daughter, Mary, who at that time was playing with a summer theater group in Maine in a play entitled *Ceiling Zero.* By a strange coincidence, the drama has for its climax a fatal airplane crash.

THE CRASH

Back at Point Barrow, Sergeant Morgan dashed to his radio key to tell the world of the tragedy. His report, as wirelessed to the War Department at Washington, gave a graphic description of the crash as obtained from Oakpeha. It read:

"At 10 P. M. last night attracted by a group of excited natives on the beach. Walking down discovered one native all out of breath gasping in pidgin English a strange tale of airplane 'she blow up.' After repeated questioning learned this native witnessed crash of an airplane at his sealing camp some fifteen miles south of Barrow and had run the entire distance to summon aid.

"Native claimed plane flying very low suddenly appeared from the south and apparently sighted tent. Plane then circled several times and finally settled upon small river near camp. Two men climbed out, one wearing 'rag on sore eye' and the other 'big man with boots.' The big man then called native to the water's edge and asked distance and direction to Point Barrow. Direction given, men then climbed back into plane and taxied off to far side of river for take-off into wind. After short run plane slowly lifted from water to height about fifty feet, banking slightly to the right when evidently motor stalled. Plane slipped off on right wing and nosed down into water, turning completely over. Native claimed dull explosion occurred and most of right wing dropped off and a film of gasoline and oil soon covered the water.

"Native frightened by explosion, turned and ran but soon controlled fright and returned, calling loudly to men in plane. Receiving no answer, then made decision to come to Barrow for help.

"With completion of the story, we knew plane to be that of Post and Rogers and quickly assembled a crew of fourteen Eskimos and departed in an open whaleboat powered with small gas motor. Hampered by recent ice floes and strong, adverse current, took nearly three hours to reach destination. Dense fog with semidarkness gave upturned plane most ghostly appearance and our hearts chilled at the thought of what we might find there. As we approached nearer the plane, we realized that no human could possibly survive the terrific crash. The plane was but a huge mass of twisted and broken wood and metal.

"The natives by this time had managed to cut into the cabin and extricate the body of Rogers, who apparently had been well back in the cabin when the plane struck and was more or less protected by the baggage carried therein. We soon learned we would have a difficult job freeing Post from the wreckage as the plane had struck with such terrific speed it had forced the engine well back into the cabin, pinning the body of Post securely. With some difficulty we managed to tear the plane apart and eventually released the body of Post. Both bodies were then carefully laid and wrapped with eider-down sleeping bags found in the wreckage and then carefully placed in the boat.

"It is believed the natives felt the loss of these two great men as keenly as we. As we started back to Barrow, one of the Eskimo boys began to sing a hymn in Eskimo and soon all voices whined in this singing and continued it until our arrival at Barrow, where we silently bore the bodies from the beach to the hospital where they were turned over to Dr. Henry Greist, who with the kindly help of Charles D. Brower prepared and dressed the bodies. It is doubtful if a person in this little village slept that night; all sat around the hospital with bowed heads with little or no talking."

"KING CHARLIE" OF THE ARCTIC

Doctor Greist, mentioned in the report, abandoned his Indiana medical practice in 1920 to go as a Presbyterian medical missionary to Alaska. Rogers and Post were on their way to visit Brower, known as "King Charlie" to the Eskimos, who had lived under the flaming lights of the aurora borealis for fifty-one years. He left his home in New York at the age of twenty-one to go to the Arctic.

2

It was only a trifling ten-minute hop from the scene of the crash to Point Barrow, but it was sufficient to bring to a violent end what had started as an aërial vacation that would have taken them leisurely around the world by way of Alaska, Siberia, China, Russia, and possibly Ethiopia. Rogers joined Post in Seattle and two days later they took off for Juneau. Post was well known in Alaska because of two flights around the world, but it was the first visit of Rogers to the country and everywhere crowds gathered to cheer him and shake his hand.

Before taking-off from Seattle, Mrs. Post, according to Rogers, asked him to take good care of Wiley, and he replied:

"Of course you mean in the air; after we get on the ground, Wiley is able to look after himself."

ROGERS IN RARE HUMOR

Rogers was in high humor on the trip. At Fairbanks, he joked about the salmon fishing of which the residents boasted.

"All these boys do is brag about who caught the biggest salmon," Will declared. "Last night an oil man brought one weighing fifty pounds to my room and wanted to put it in bed with me. I can't see the use of catching salmon when they crawl out of the water to meet you.

"The first handshake I got when I stepped ashore was from a big coho. A coho, they tell me, is a king salmon that's on relief."

After their stay at Fairbanks, Rogers and Post took to the air to fly the 500-mile stretch to Point

Barrow.   The weather was none too good when
they started, but Post decided that if they ran into
adverse conditions, they would "sit down" on one
of the numerous lakes in the barren, frost-bitten
country.   A radio report from Barrow shortly
after their departure indicated they would en-
counter fog and poor visibility over most of their
route.   Fifty miles out from Fairbanks the blind-
ing Arctic fog closed in.   Ahead of them was the
Brooks Range with its snow-capped peaks.   They
dared not go on.   Post brought the plane down on
Harding Lake and waited for the weather to clear.
They were impatient to be on the way and as soon
as the visibility lifted, they decided to try it.   On the
wing again they chose to poke their way through
the fog in order to reach Point Barrow.   When
they figured they were close to their destination,
they came down close to the ground in the hope of
finding some landmark that would show them the
way.   When he saw the Eskimo's camp, Post
decided to land and ask the way to Point Barrow.

The missing of Point Barrow was no reflection on
Post's ability as an aërial navigator.   Veteran
fliers, who had flown the route numerous times,
lost their bearings on several occasions when they
encountered fog and, if anything, it was a tribute to
Post's skill that he came within fifteen miles of his
objective.   During the brief stop on the tundra
river, Wiley tinkered with the engine and Will
"gabbed" with the Eskimo—as might be expected.
Undoubtedly, from that lone seal hunter, Rogers
found material for a jest that he intended to relate

sometime, for everywhere he went he saw something with a humorous twist in it.

Even his taciturn flying companion was a fitting subject, and in one of his last pieces of writing he said of Post: "Wiley is kinder of a Calvin Coolidge on answers. None of 'em are going to bother you with being too long."

After obtaining the direction to Point Barrow, Post sent the plane across the river for a take-off into the wind. Flying speed across the water!

What happened? No one knows. Whatever it was, it was beyond the skill of any flier to overcome, for Wiley Post was rated as one of the greatest pilots that ever lived. An air lock in the gasoline feed line or the sudden freezing of the carburetor, due to the failure of the super-heater to act promptly, has been suggested as the cause. The engine quit and without sufficient height it was impossible to bring the ship under control.

ARCTIC FLIGHT HAZARDOUS

Flying in the Arctic, where such noted pilots as Carl Ben Eielson and Frank Dorbandt perished, is a terrible ordeal at all times, according to flying men who have braved its hazards many times. In the region of Point Barrow, there is ice and snow most of the year and in the few weeks of summer there is soft sand to make it difficult to take-off and land. Fog and mist arise suddenly to blind the flier and throw him off his course. And as for storms, the fliers call northern Alaska "the breeding ground of cyclones."

Joe Crosson, hero of many an Arctic flight, advised the two vacationists to remain at Fairbanks until the weather cleared before hopping off for Point Barrow, but Post and Rogers were long accustomed to flying as a matter of everyday business and they faced the hazards in a spirit of fun.

"If we meet bad weather," said Rogers, "we'll just set down, cpen a can of chili, and throw a party until it clears."

And so their red ship roared into the mist at Fairbanks and disappeared to the north. Crosson watched them depart, and as a flier his thought was of the plane.

"There's a ship to go places with," he said. "With that engine, Wiley could lift her out of a frog pond."

The thermometer registered 45 degrees at the time of their start and there were reports of dense fog along the way. But Crosson felt no concern, for he felt that the plane, as well made and as powerfully engined as it was, in the hands of a flier like Wiley Post could get through regardless of fog.

Before leaving for Point Barrow, Rogers had told friends in Alaska that after going to Siberia, they planned to go to strange places and eventually come back to America by way of Iceland and Greenland. Their longest water jump by the indefinite route they had outlined was about 1,000 miles, but Rogers seemed to think little of that. Crosson did not agree with them. He was of the opinion that such a long flight over water was a grave hazard.

"OFF FOR SOMEWHERE"

There was something almost prophetic in one of the last articles Rogers wrote before his death. It was entitled "Off for Somewhere in a Red Bus." "Off for somewhere——!" The words seem to envision the tragic ending on the tundra.

But both men died as they wished. Post, in commenting on his pioneering flights into the stratosphere, once said: "I know it's dangerous. But if I get popped off, that's the way I want to go—doing the things I want to do." Once it had been arranged to carry Rogers on a night flight from Dallas to Chicago in a mail plane. He declined to ride in the plane under a waiver when he learned that the plane was not authorized to carry passengers. He chartered a plane and followed the mail plane to Chicago.

"We should not break the rules," Rogers commented. "And then, too, I would have had to have ridden on a parachute if I had flown in the mail plane. Picture this farm boy dangling from a parachute. I'll always come in with the plane."

In a speech he made in Boston in 1930, Rogers told of the epitaph he wanted placed on his grave.

"When I die," he said, "my epitaph, or whatever you call those signs on gravestones, is going to read: 'I joked about every prominent man of my time, but I never met a man I didn't like.'

"I am proud of that. I can hardly wait to die so it can be carved. And when you come around to my grave, you'll probably find me sitting there proudly reading it."

CHAPTER II

Rogers' Boyhood

WHEN Will Rogers first saw the light of day in a ranch house in the old Indian Territory, now the State of Oklahoma, his mother, a devout Methodist, hoped he would grow up to become a minister of the Gospel. She cherished this dream until he ran away from home, which caused a relative to prophesy that young Will was destined to be hanged as a horse thief. Neither of these expectations, of course, materialized, and no one foresaw that the drawling, loose-jointed cowboy was ordained to become a preacher of the finest kind of doctrine, the best loved American of his time and the favorite of statesmen, presidents, and kings.

Will Rogers was born November 4, 1879. Jokingly, he used to claim that his birthday was an Election Day and that it gave him the natural right to poke fun at those who sat in the high chancelleries of government all over the world. His own explanation of the place of his birth was "halfway between Claremore and Oologah, before there was a town in either place." He claimed Claremore for convenience, he said, because "nobody but an Indian can pronounce Oologah." His parents, Clement Vann Rogers and Mary Schrimpsher Rogers, both had Cherokee Indian blood in their veins. They came from pioneer stock. Those two facts were a great satisfaction to Rogers in his later life and he frequently remarked, "My ancestors didn't come over in the *Mayflower*—they met the boat."

FATHER AN INDIAN TRADER

Will's father fought in the Civil War as an officer on the Confederate side, and afterwards operated a trading post where he dealt profitably with the Osage Indians. He quit trading to become a cattle man. Of his parents, Rogers once said:

"My father was one eighth Cherokee and my mother one fourth Cherokee, which I figure makes me about one eighth cigar-store Injun."

Regardless of genetics and the Mendelian Law, Will Rogers undoubtedly drew upon all three strains, Irish, Scotch, and American Indian, to fashion the character that was so beloved by the world. From the Irish came his sense of humor, roguish as it was, and his great, generous heart. The Scotch added a keen sense of business and forthrightness, and from the Indian came the dignity and reserve that prevented him as the Nation's jester from descending to the level of a merry-andrew.

Will was impressively baptized William Penn Adair Rogers, the only boy among six girls in the family. His first callers as he lay in his cradle in the comfortable ranch house were the cowboys from the Rogers' ranch. A miniature of the house was built by the school children of Oologah in honor of Rogers in 1930. It stands on a plot in the center of the town.

At Claremore, a few years before Rogers' death, the Pocahontas Club, an Indian organization, of which he was an honorary member, fêted Will Rogers at a dinner. Among the guests was one of the cowboys, who had seen Will shortly after his birth. The cowboy, dressed in a range riding outfit with leather chaps, stood in a corner as Oklahoma's most famous native son came into the banquet hall. Rogers looked at the white-haired old plainsman and recognized him immediately. He rushed over to him.

"Barney, you old rascal, how are you gettin' along?"

The old man recalled how he had seen Will when he was only six weeks old.

"I realized then," Barney declared, "you would never take a prize in a beauty contest. Your mother looked up at me. I can see her smile now. She said: 'Barney, I know what you're thinkin'. He isn't much for looks, but I know he's going to be one of the best boys that ever lived."

Tears shone in Rogers' blue eyes.

"There was something mighty peculiar about that first time I saw you," said the old cowboy.

"What was that?" asked Will.

"You were speechless."

The joke sent Rogers into a spasm of laughter. He thoroughly enjoyed being on the receiving end of a good gag for once in his life.

Rogers often pretended he did not know the exact date of his birth, and from the standpoint of show business it was a shrewd thing not to reveal one's exact age.

"Well," Will told an interviewer one day, "I was born, of course, you've got to be born—that's about the only thing you have to do to get on the stage. I don't know what year the great event took place, but I am supposed to be a good many years on the trail. I was born the year after the cattle had died from the blizzard in our country and any old longhorn will tell you when that was."

THAT BIRTH CERTIFICATE

One of Will Rogers' best stories, of which there are numerous versions, had to do with the question of a birth certificate as prerequisite for a passport to Europe. A young lady clerk, according to Will, presented him with an application blank to fill out and an affidavit to be sworn to by someone concerning the place of his birth.

"I told her," he said, "that I had no birth certificate; and as for someone present at my birth and can swear to it, I think that's going to be rather difficult. You know the old-time ladies of which I am a direct descendant were of a retiring nature and being born was a private affair, not a public function.

"In the early days of the Indian Territory, where I was born, there were no such things as birth certificates. You being there was certificate enough. We generally took it for granted if you were there you must have been born. That was about the only thing we didn't dispute. Having a certificate of being born was like wearing a raincoat in the water over a bathing suit."

Will finally solved the difficulty when a friend volunteered to swear to the affidavit. The friend said he knew Will's father well.

"Now, he had never been west of the Hudson River," said Rogers, "and my father had never been east of the Mississippi, so it was one of the longest distance friendships on record. I thought it was funny he never mentioned knowing father before to me."

Will's father, whom he called "The Chief," was moderately well-to-do and stood high in the cow country. The elder Rogers was a member of the convention that drafted the Oklahoma State Constitution and a county was named for him. Will often laughed at that. He said:

"Shucks, they had to change the name. Nobody could pronounce the old one—Cooweescoowee."

BORN BOWLEGGED

By the time he was five years old, Will Rogers could ride a horse and he often said that "like other Oklahoma kids, I was born bowlegged so I could set on a horse." The infant also twirled a rope in imitation of his elders and he gained remarkable proficiency, so much so that when he was fourteen, he was rated as a top cow hand and roper. He gained that recognition when he entered a rodeo in competition with older cowboys and won a riding and roping contest. Rogers loved horses and the wild, free life of the open range, but his father and mother planned that their son should have more than the desultory schooling which the territory afforded. It must have been a sad day indeed for the fun-loving boy when he was told he must quit the rolling prairie for the restricted campus of a boarding school. Will was sent to a school at Neosho, Missouri, where, it seems, the only thing for which he distinguished himself was an imitation of a colored preacher. This was given on Friday afternoons at the recitation period by popular demand. He next went to the Kemper Military Academy, at Boonville, in the same state, only to remain "a little while."

"I went to pretty nearly every school in the country for a little while," Rogers used to say, "except West Point. I could have gone there, too, only I was too proud to talk to a Congressman."

AT MILITARY SCHOOL

But life at the military school with its strict regulations and form-fitting tunics must have been the last straw for the restless youth from the plains, for he wrote his father that he was going to "skip school and help some fellers dig an oil well in Texas." The elder Rogers told him to go ahead and "work out his own salvation." Digging for oil proved an irksome task, and Will bombarded his home with letters telling of the privations in the oil fields and his homesickness for the ranch. His father laughed at the letters and then when he decided the son had been taught a lesson, sent him money to come home.

Back at the ranch, "The Chief" told Willie, as he called him, that his school days were over and that it was high time he had taken over some of the responsibility of the ranch. The elder Rogers named his son steward of the ranch and gave him the power of attorney on the family bank account. The father then left on a business trip. The first thing Will proceeded to do was build a dance platform, where he staged dancing and roping contests. It was all a celebration, Will said, of his return home and the end of his confining school days. In all, he spent about $1,000 of his father's money and that was "a pile of money in them days." Young Rogers won many of the dancing prizes because of his skill at strutting the cakewalk, which was then coming into vogue in that section of the country. The storm broke when his father returned. The power of attorney was revoked and Will was thrown upon his own resources.

RIDING THE RANGE

Undaunted, the youth saddled a pony and rode away. On a near-by ranch he found work as a cow hand, and one of his first tasks was helping in the dehorning of 3,000 steers. Years later, Percy Gassaway, Congressman from Oklahoma and a former cowboy, told of working on that ranch, which was owned by Colonel W. P. Ewing. Gassaway said he noticed a youth sitting on the fence of the corral doing nothing but cracking jokes all the time. Finally, Gassaway asked Ewing:

"Why is he staying around?"

Colonel Ewing laughed and replied:

"In the first place, he's so funny I can't let him go, and in the second place, I'm just wondering if he'll ever do anything."

Eventually his father forgot the "celebration" over the ending of Will's school days and took him back into the good graces of the family. He was given a herd of cattle of his own and he raised them until they were worth $12,000. Then Rogers' vagabond spirit began to itch the soles of his feet and he longed to be on the way to far-away places. He was twenty-one when he sold his herd and with another young cowboy started for the Argentine.

"When a fellow ain't got much mind," Will commented years later, "it don't take him long to make it up."

The pair of youthful adventurers went to New Orleans where they hoped to get a boat for the South American cow country, but they were advised to go to New York. On arriving there they were told that "this year's boat for Buenos Aires" had gone, and it was suggested that they go to England where there was a regular line to the Argentine. They went that way, but Rogers was seasick most of the journey and his diet for the entire trip, he said later, was a couple of lemons.

THE FLIP OF A COIN

Eventually, the two got jobs "punching" cattle on the pampas for the equivalent of $4.20 a month. This was not anything like the rosy dreams with which they had started out from Oklahoma, and by that time most of the money Rogers had obtained from the sale of his cattle was gone. Will's buddy developed a bad case of homesickness and there was only enough money to pay the fare home for one of them.

They flipped a coin and Rogers' companion won. Will remained behind, working with the gauchos. Of that time Rogers relates the following:

"I was sorter itching to show these gauchos how I could rope and tie down a steer. One day they wanted to catch one to put the brand on him, so I takes down my little manila rope. I even went so far as to pick out the exact spot I was going to lay the steer down.

"Well, I hadn't even got close enough to start swinging my rope when I heard something go whizzing over my head. A guy running about twenty feet behind me had thrown clear over my head and caught the steer. Why, he could rope a steer better'n I could shoot a guy with a Winchester."

GOES TO BOER WAR

Meanwhile, the Boer War was being fought in South Africa and young Rogers longed to go there. Broke, but still smiling and wisecracking, he got a job on a cattle boat as valet to a cargo of mules to Capetown.

"They were almost tame and didn't kick—much," laughed Rogers in reminiscing about those days.

At Ladysmith, he got a job at a remount station breaking horses. Shortly after this, the war came to a close and the youthful wanderer was broke once more. In speaking of his service in the Boer War, Rogers frequently declared the war ended the day he landed in South Africa, but that was one of his countless jests.

Rogers heard that an American showman, named Texas Jack, was at Johannesburg with his one-ring circus and Wild West Show. Will made his way to the town and found Texas Jack outside the tent doing a comparatively simple rope trick known as "spinning out." The showman offered $100 to any member of the crowd who could duplicate the feat. It looked like easy money to the Oklahoma cowboy and he hurried to the show platform. There he picked up the rope, slouched over the edge of the platform, and with his blue eyes twinkling and his mouth twisted up in his familiar grin "spun out" just as Texas had done. Then he threw in a few intricate tricks for good measure. The crowd thought it was part of the show and applauded enthusiastically. But to Rogers it meant $100 and when he asked for it, he found it was all a bluff. Texas Jack didn't have 100 dimes at that moment, but he offered Will a job with the show doing fancy riding and roping. Any "chuck wagon" to which he could attach himself looked good to him at the minute and he accepted the job with alacrity, without much caring that he was starting on a career as a showman which was to be unequaled by anyone in his lifetime.

"THE CHEROKEE KID"

He was billed as "The Cherokee Kid" and from the beginning was the star attraction of the show. From Africa, he worked his way with the show to New Zealand and Australia, where he joined the Wirth Show, owned by Mae Wirth's father. Mae later became one of the greatest bareback riders in the history of the circus. With this show, Rogers went to Japan and China and eventually landed in San Francisco. This was three years after he had started out to see the world.

"From San Francisco," Will said, "I bummed my way back to Oologah and I heard a feller tell my dad he didn't think I had done so well because I came home wearin' overalls for underwear."

Then followed one of his occasional "resting" periods and Rogers always described himself as "one of the most accomplished resters on earth." But after his experiences, the cow town of Oologah, with its dusty roads, tiny collection of stores, hitching racks, and plank sidewalks, looked good to the young traveler. It was a welcome haven where three good meals were forthcoming daily.

Will Rogers' indifferent education in his youth supplied him with much material for many of his best quips and his most famous line was: "Sure I studied McGuffey's Fourth Reader for ten years." Rogers liked that one and, showman that he was, he embellished it as the years went by.

The next time he used it, he drawled:

"I studied McGuffey's Fourth Reader for ten years. In the end I knew more about it than McGuffey."

DRESSING UP A JOKE

After a few more versions, it finally became quite an anecdote:

"My father was pretty well fixed, and I being the only male son, he tried terribly hard to make

3

something out of me. He sent me to about every school in that part of the country. In some of them, I would last for three or four months. I got just as far as the fourth reader when the teachers wouldn't seem to be running the school right, and rather than have the school stop, I would generally leave.

"Then I would start in another school, tell them I had just finished the third reader and was ready for the fourth.

"Well, I knew all this fourth grade by heart, so the teacher would say:

"'I never see you studying, yet you seem to know your lessons.'

"I had that education thing figured down to a fine point. Ten years in McGuffey's Fourth Reader and I knew more about it than McGuffey did."

It was his delight to joke about his laggard days in school, and undoubtedly he was not much of a student but he could always make the class laugh when called upon to recite. Underneath Will Rogers' mask of "ignorance" was a well-mannered and cultured man with a shrewd, trained mind. He might have had college degrees to add to his name had he so desired. Dr. Nicholas Murray Butler, president of Columbia University, met Rogers during an ocean voyage and became so impressed by his wit and wisdom that he told the former he would call him to Columbia to receive an honorary degree.

Will grinned sheepishly and drawled:

"Well, Doctor Butler, I know they give college degrees for pretty nearly every kind of ignorance but I didn't know they gave any for my kind."

REFUSES COLLEGE DEGREES

Other colleges sought to confer honors upon Rogers, but he refused them all. One of the reasons for this was that he was extremely modest and refused to believe that he was as great as he really was.

In later years, as Will Rogers climbed the dizzy heights of fame where his advice was sought by the Nation's leaders, someone circulated the report that he was not the simple "ignerant cowboy" he said he was but had actually been graduated from Oxford University. At first he smiled at the story but as it went the rounds and many accepted it as a fact, Will became much embarrassed. He finally exploded the rumor with one of his barbed shafts of wit:

"It's a base canard," he said. "Nothin' to it. Shucks, I always thought Oxford was the name of a shoe until I went to England a couple of years ago and they dragged me out to look at the college."

While on the subject of education, Will could always find some utterance that would cause a laugh but which contained a large kernel of wisdom. In the days when the college boys were going in for "plus-four" knickers and Oxford bags, Rogers took one look at them and chuckled:

"What the youth of this country needs is narrower pants and broader ideas."

And once while commenting on higher education he declared:

"College is wonderful because it takes the children away from home just as they reach the arguing stage."

On another occasion a committee of citizens from
Oklahoma came to Will and asked him to run for
Congress and he replied:

"At old Willie Halsell College I studied elocution
for a while and if I hadn't given it up then, I might
take up your proposition now.   In fact, I gave it
up because I was afraid I'd get to be a Senator."

GIFT OF GAB

Much of the cowboy's wit was on topics of the
day and it perished with the day.   He viewed his
own "gift of gab" humorously as was shown on
the occasion when asked to run for Governor of
Oklahoma against his old friend, Governor "Alfalfa
Bill" Murray.

"I won't run this time," he said, "though running
in Oklahoma used to be about the best thing I did.
When I was a kid in school, my nickname was
'Rabbit' because I was so fast on my feet.   A boy
that gabbed as much about things that were none
of his business as I did had to be fast on his feet."

The citizens of Oklahoma, however, found a way
to pay him honor when a new six-story hotel was
built in Claremore.   They named the structure
Will Rogers Hotel and called him back to the
town to help dedicate it.   After inspecting it, Will
remarked, "Why this has more bathrooms than
Buckingham Palace."

"When I was a kid in this town," he continued,
"I used to envy General Grant and Jesse James
because they had cigars named after them.   But,
shucks, I've got it on them now."

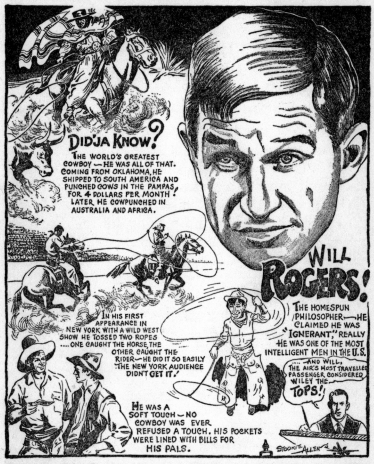

This cartoon by Stookie Allen appeared in a recent edition of the New York *Daily Mirror*. It attracted universal attention and admiration. The Smithsonian Institution at Washington requested of the artist the original drawing to be preserved among its archives. It is an excellent portrayal of the life of Will Rogers.

CHAPTER III

A Cowboy's Courtship

THE YOUNGER generation of the little, frontier cow town of Oologah was in a fever of excitement when Will Rogers arrived home after his travels in South Africa, the Antipodes, and the Orient but the agitation was not occasioned by the return of the prodigal. No fatted calf was slaughtered in honor of his coming, for the meanderings of cowboys were taken for granted and for all it mattered, Will might just as well have been working in the neighboring county. The flurry was caused by a pretty girl with whom Will proceeded to fall in love at first sight but he was too shy even to seek an introduction. She was Betty Blake, a young lady in her 'teens and the sister of the Oologah depot agent. She had come to the little town on a visit from her home in Arkansas.

The bicycle craze was just sweeping the country, and young Rogers was one of the first in his section to procure one. A born showman, he decided on a campaign to win the young lady's attention. Miss Blake was seated on her porch one day when Will came tearing down the dusty road on his new two-wheeler. He planned to show her some trick riding just as he had seen cyclists perform in his travels. Something went wrong, for the trick ended in mid-air and Will landed on his head. Betty rushed to his aid and as she wiped the blood from a slight cut, he grinned and drawled, "Guess I'd better stick to cow ponies."

That was the beginning, and thereafter the courtship was conducted in a rubber-tired buggy. In later years Rogers always smilingly declared that he wore out a set of the tires driving Betty around trying to get her to say "yes." At any rate, Betty left for her home in Rogers, Arkansas, where she became a school teacher and Will went back trouping with a Wild West show which he joined in Oklahoma. From there he went on to "big-time" vaudeville and with a comfortable salary assured, Rogers thought once more of the pretty girl he had left behind him in the Southwest. The beauties he met along Broadway and in show business meant nothing to him. Rogers was part of the glamorous night life of New York's most brilliant period but he did not belong to it. In November, 1908, he hurried down to Arkansas and there took the bride who was to be his only partner and sweetheart through the years that he was climbing from a cow-hand vaudeville performer to a place of international fame. The ceremony was performed in the modest two-story frame house where the young schoolteacher made her home.

"It was the luckiest thing that ever happened to me," Rogers frequently declared. "Betty is to blame for it all. Whatever I am or have accomplished, I owe to Betty. I ain't got no sense. My wife made me what I am. In other words—local girl makes good in the city—makes good man."

THE PERFECT MATCH

In the hurly-burly of the theatrical world where divorce was a common occurrence the Rogers marriage was classed as the "perfect match." Just before his death, Will commented on his stardom in the movies: "I'm not a real movie star. I still got the same wife I started out with nearly twenty-eight years ago."

And three days after his death, Mrs. Rogers received the last expression of his affection for her. It was a small package addressed to her at Beverly Hills, California. The name and address were written in the careless, rambling scrawl that was Will's typical handwriting. In the box was a small red fox fur, a souvenir of the country where he met his end. It was sent from Juneau, Alaska, the first stop made by Rogers and Post on their tragic flight.

From the day of their marriage, Mrs. Rogers, a tall, blonde, blue-eyed, and gracious woman took charge of Will. She mothered his children and made home the dearest spot on earth to all of them, whether it was the extensive ranch at Santa Monica or their simple bungalow at Beverly Hills. Self-effacing and understanding, she never interfered in her husband's career but undoubtedly she was the one guiding genius that did the most to help him along the path to greatness. A lesser character could have blighted the sturdy oak that was Will Rogers.

"Betty," Will told cronies, "is my manager. I try to get in a few laughs and get some money and then let her do the rest. She is the financial end of the firm."

When guests came to their home, Will always acted as if they had come to call on her rather than himself.

"Oh, sometimes they come out to see me," he said proudly, "but when they go away, they remember only Betty."

WIFE'S JUDGMENT BEST

It was her judgment that Will trusted above all others. Whenever a new contract was to be signed, he never put a pen to the paper until he had first consulted his wife. He would stuff it in his pocket, according to Winfield Sheehan, his boss at the Fox studios, with the remark, "You know I've got to see someone about this."

Will read her every word he wrote at home before sending it out for publication. If she failed to understand some reference to politics, he would change it because he reasoned that others might miss the point. If the writing was supposed to be humorous and it failed to amuse her, Will would throw it away and try again. He read all the newspapers in the town at breakfast and threw them on the floor as fast as he had finished with them. He couldn't pack a grip and was certain to miss trains unless Mrs. Rogers bossed the job, and he was always late for meals except at breakfast. He was an early riser, getting along with seven hours' sleep or less.

In an interview, Mrs. Rogers was once asked to describe Will at home. The result was a vivid picture of Will Rogers, the husband and father.

"Is Will funny at home?" she said, repeating the first question put to her. "Of course he is! Will can't help being funny no matter where he happens to be. His humor isn't the artificial kind that you can put on and take off like a coat. He's just himself. He's always himself. He doesn't try to be funny. He just is."

ROGERS AT HOME

"But anyone who thinks that Will at home is constantly the entertainer, is very much mistaken. He works hard and much of his time is taken up by reading. When he comes home after a long or short absence, we all rush to him, crowd about him. Everything is gay and joyous. But he isn't the type that slips into a dressing gown and slippers and relaxes. He is too busy for that and much too active. When he isn't writing or reading or sleeping or eating, he's riding horseback with the children.

"Hero worship isn't one of his tendencies and he is never particularly impressed by anybody. The statesmen and other great men he met he judged simply as good, bad, or indifferent people. I don't mean that Will doesn't recognize greatness in people but he doesn't change his own personality to suit others."

Will's devotion to his wife and children was always the greatest thing in his life. They had three children, Will, Jr., who was twenty-three when his father died; Mary, two years younger; and Jimmy, two years farther down the line. Another son, who died in infancy, was named Fred after Fred Stone, musical comedy star and one of Rogers' best friends. Will was never cross with the children and he never spanked them.

"I had to take care of the spankings," Mrs. Rogers once said.

CHILDREN GOOD RIDERS

The Rogers children before they could walk were placed upon a horse's back and taught to ride. In 1917 they caused considerable comment when they appeared on horseback at an outdoor show.

"New Yorkers," wrote the New York *Sun*, "who went to the big benefit at the Polo Grounds last summer for the Sun Tobacco Fund will remember the amazement the little tykes created when they came galloping out, yipping and sticking to the leather like regular cow men. Their pa wasn't any prouder of them that day than he is every day, because whenever he thinks of, talks to, or sees, those kids, he just naturally throws his pride into high and breaks all the speed laws on the statute books."

Rogers, himself, wrote the captions for the pictures of his children that were taken at that time. They reveal Will's flair for writing succinct paragraphs with a touch of humor. At the same time they show how proud he was of his youngsters. The captions follow:

"Youngest cowboy in the world, Jim, age two, and he can ride. If you want to start a Civil War, just try to take him off that pony. He eats there."

"All mounted on their own ponies. The youngest cow terrors in the world. Bill, six, and Mary, four."

"Here we come, all in a dead run, and nobody holding on. They won't ride unless they can ride in a run. I'm riding the only opposition to a Ford."

"The Home Defense League on parade. The tough little bird on the end is not holding his gun right, but none of us has the nerve to tell him so. That's Roosevelt Rogers."

THE ROGERS RANCH

Will loved every foot of his ranch because it gave him an opportunity to play and ride with his children. On the place he kept more than 100 head of horses, many of them tough little polo ponies. The ranch also was a tribute to his business sagacity. The first section of it cost $3,000 and represented his first investment in California real estate. When he died, the ranch was valued at more than $500,000. He had two polo fields on the place and was credited with introducing the game to the movie colony.

Rogers never stopped talking, even while playing a fast game of polo. When he was charging down on the ball with a cowboy yell, he was telling some-one else how to smack the willow sphere. He rode hard and was in nearly every play. One of his favorite tricks was to crowd his opponent's horse and force the animal to veer away from the ball. Despite his age, he played a fearless game and while he didn't have many spills, he was whacked in the face several times with a mallet while dashing into the play.

One of the best polo teams on the ranch was composed of Will, his two sons, and Mary. They played some splendid games until Mary, as her father put it, "left and went society on us."

For the most part, however, Will kept his children in the background and refused to let them be exploited because of his fame. Once they showed the inclination to strike out in the world for themselves and proved their ability to take care of themselves, he sat proudly back and let them go ahead.

"They are not the kinda kids who want to get by on anything I may have done," he declared. "And I won't let anyone exploit them simply because they are my kids."

MARY SEEKS STAGE CAREER

Mary's decision to seek a stage and screen career was, in her father's words, "her own doin's." When she was nineteen, she sought out David Butler, director, and B. G. DeSylva, Fox producer, when she heard they were casting for a musical comedy movie and asked for a job. She introduced herself as Mary Blake and made a successful screen test. She was put to work before either they or her father discovered her little plot. Will was proud of her achievement but he refused to help her with her career. However, he did not interfere when she went East to dramatic school and was happy at her success in the plays in which she had a part with summer stock companies. Mary continued to use her mother's name and went on with the tedious process of "learning to act" by joining the Lake Players at Skowhegan, Maine, where she played two summer seasons.

By a strange coincidence, she was playing the feminine lead in an aviation play, *Ceiling Zero*, when her father crashed in the Arctic. In the play, the leading man, "father" of the girl portrayed by Mary Rogers, was killed in an airplane crash. This was the climax of the play.

A few days before the accident, Rogers sent the following telegram to his daughter as a word of encouragement:

"Since I wired you last year for the opening of the Lakewood Theater I got up there and seen the place. It's awful pretty. You got no reason for not acting good there. Give all the actors and folks up there my love. Tell Mr. Burke, the director, not to take the play too seriously, as the Supreme Court is liable to rule it illegal, anyhow.

"I expect there is quite a few Republicans showing their heads this year. It's been one of the best seasons for them in four or five years. I will be up to see you, but not till the snow starts melting."

Rogers attended Mary's début as an actress in New York in the winter of 1934. As he described the play, it had a "successful run on the stage of one consecutive week." He went back stage to congratulate her after the performance and while waiting with Mrs. Rogers to go into her dressing room, a fireman passed them.

"Now, there's a job that must be rather nice," Mrs. Rogers said.

"Oh, I don't know," drawled Will. "He never gets to any fires and think of all the actors he has to listen to."

PROUD OF ELDEST SON

Will also was proud of the fact that his eldest son, whom he called Bill, refused to trade on his father's name and was determined to make his own way in the newspaper business. Eventually, the young man told his father, he hoped to buy and publish a country newspaper; the dream, incidentally, of every newspaper man since the discovery of printer's ink. Will teased the boy about it occasionally.

"You couldn't ever write like your pappy, anyway," he told him.

"Maybe not," replied Bill, "but when I get to be a publisher, I can hire plenty of men to do the writing."

Will Rogers was always thinking about his children and worried about their safety when they were away from home. During the winter of 1933 a heavy downpour of rain washed out the road leading to the Rogers ranch. A deep gully made the road impassable and motorists that crashed into it were certain to be killed. It was New Year's Eve and the Rogers children were out at a party. Will saddled a horse and lighted a red lantern. With the water swishing up his horse's knees, Rogers patrolled the road near the chasm all night warning motorists of their danger. He kept at his task with fear clutching at his heart for he knew that if this one road were washed out, others were likely to be.

Finally, young Bill came driving up and saw the red lantern swinging in the rain. Then he heard his father shout: "H'ya there! Stop your car!"

When he saw his son, he shook hands with him and shouted, "Bill, I'm sho' glad you made it."

Rogers never believed in investing money in stocks and bonds. He used to say: "I'll take mine in good old mother earth. A feller can have some fun fixing a spot for himself and his family and his friends to enjoy in this life."

WILL A TIRELESS "FIXER"

He was a tireless "fixer" and the story is told of his remodeling of a home he once owned in Beverly Hills. He decided it was time that Mary had her own suite of bedroom, sitting room, and bath. A contractor was called in and the plans were made. But every time Rogers came home, he wanted something changed. This room was moved and that torn down. The poor builder was in despair and no one had any notion of what the place would be like if it ever was completed. Will solved the problem after all when he ordered:

"Tear the whole blamed thing down."

At the Santa Monica ranch home, Will was always making changes in the sprawling, rambling place with its great rooms and comfortable furniture. In the ranch house he had private quarters for himself, including a room filled with souvenirs

from all parts of the globe, all of them gifts from
the great and near-great whom he had met on his
travels.   One room was devoted entirely to Indian
things, many of them priceless, for the Indians
regarded Rogers as the greatest of men.

The latest addition to the ranch was a two-
room log cabin, half a mile away from the main
house and reached only by a rough bridle trail.
This was Will's exclusive, private haven.   He had
it decorated with Indian trappings in the gay
color schemes that marked the old pueblos of the
Southwest.

On one occasion, Will was showing a visitor
around the ranch.   He pointed out some adjoining
properties and said: "See those pretty white fences?
Every one of them surrounds a mortgage."

RESTLESS AROUND HOME

Around the house, he was restless, moving from
chair to chair.   He was always fiddling with something and if lunch was late, he would pick up two
forks and bang them for service.   At one time or
another he bought a hurdy-gurdy, piano, violin,
banjo, drums, mandolin, and guitar.   He could
pick out a few chords on the guitar but only because
they had been pointed out to him and he had
laboriously learned them for a part in a show in
which he was starred.   He tried to pick out tunes
on the others but was successful only with the
hurdy-gurdy.

Nothing could be as eloquent and as revealing of
his innate modesty as the incident that occurred

4

when he took Mrs. Rogers for an automobile ride. They decided to stop at a motion-picture theater. Before reaching the box office, Will discovered he had no money with him. Mrs. Rogers' handbag likewise was empty.

"Let's go home, Betty," he said.

And they did. It apparently never occurred to him that he need only appear at any theater in the United States and a good part of Europe besides, to be given immediate entrance without stopping for a ticket. Not only that, but one of his pictures was being shown on the screen of the theater that he had wanted to attend.

CHAPTER IV

ROGERS ON THE STAGE

AFTER the fun and excitement of traveling with a circus in the Antipodes and the Orient, the thought of staying on the range "punching" Oklahoma cattle was not very appealing to Will Rogers and he longed to be on the open road showing his skill to the applauding crowds. As he expressed it:

"I was spoiled by that time. It seemed plumb unnatural to punch cows without an audience."

Even though he returned home "broke," he found something to laugh at in the experience years later when he was a success on Broadway, and his earning capacity far greater than the most avaricious dreams of his youth.

"Guess I've got a claim to the round-the-world booby prize," he declared, "as it had taken me almost three years to land in Frisco, broke. The moral of this story is: always get a round-trip ticket. It's cheaper in the long run."

Zach Mulhall, of Oklahoma, was organizing a Wild West Show at that time. Will returned from his travels and he signed on. The outfit trouped through the Southwest and then went to the World's Fair at St. Louis in 1904. Among Will's fellow troupers were Tom Mix, Zach Miller, later the owner of Miller Brothers' 101 Ranch Wild West Show, and

Lucille Mulhall, the boss's daughter and the first woman rodeo performer. The following year the outfit moved into the old Madison Square Garden in New York to give the effete East an exhibition of real riding and roping. Twenty-six-year-old Will Rogers was the star roper of the show and he had the opportunity to show that it was more than mere showmanship.

ROPES WILD STEER

One night one of the steers used in the roping act ran wild and jumped over the railing of the arena into the crowd. As the frightened spectators dashed up the stairs, the steer was about to charge into them. Rogers, who had seen the animal start its mad dash, coiled up his lariat as he ran across the tanbark. Swish! The snaky coil of manila flew through the air and settled over the head of the enraged animal. Will dug the high heels of his cowboy boots into the tanbark and leaned back on the rope. He choked all the fight out of the steer and then led him back to the temporary corral in the Garden. The next day, Will Rogers found himself proclaimed a hero on the front pages of all the New York newspapers. After reading the accounts, Will was seized with a new ambition and that was to stay in New York. When the Mulhall show left town, Rogers remained behind looking for a vaude-ville booking. But single cowboy acts were unheard of and it was tough sledding before he was finally hired to do a supper show at the Union Square Theater.

Air view of Will Rogers' ranch, showing the riding ring, the polo stable, and the Western stable.

The roping corral on Will Rogers' ranch in Southern California.

Will Rogers claimed that he had an ideal polo team until "Mary took to Society."

"The supper show," Rogers explained afterward, "meant that all the big acts did two shows a day and the little ones an extra at supper time between six and eight when nobody that had a home or somewhere to eat would be in the theater."

In vaudeville, Rogers did not take his audiences by storm at the outset. He trouped on the Klaw & Erlanger circuit, opening and closing the shows. His was strictly a "dumb" act. He had yet to find that his greatest talent was in the ready wit with which he amused stagehands and fellow players.

ROGERS STARTS TO TALK

Many persons have claimed they were the first to persuade Rogers to change from a "dumb" part to a monolog. Most of the claims, however, were without foundation, for above everything else, Will Rogers was inherently a showman. In his vaudeville days he used to put on his act and then stand in the "entrance" to the stage studying the other acts that were put on. He was in love with the theater and he wanted to excel in it. It did not take him long to realize that laughs—not physical skill—produce the most money in the show business. Rogers was not long in realizing that what he needed in his bit was a few wisecracks. It probably happened that Rogers missed one of his tricks at a performance, and to fill in the awkward pause that followed before it was repeated, he attempted a quip over the mishap. Many performers in vaudeville intentionally missed tricks for the express purpose of making some comment, and it was not likely that

Rogers was slow in adopting their technique. He was, however, modest and shy to an extreme and that may have held him back for a time, but eventually he added more and more talking to the act. It did not catch on with audiences at the start and sometimes he was content just to present his roping act.

In his early act, Rogers used a lariat, a white horse, and a rider as properties. As the orchestra played "Cheyenne," Will would shuffle down to the center of the stage with a rope in each hand. The horse and rider would come galloping out of the wings across the stage and in the twinkling of an eye, Rogers would throw the rope in his right hand around the horse and the one in his left hand around the rider. It was a difficult trick but it was executed so swiftly that the spectators could not appreciate what had happened. A fellow actor told Rogers that if he would stop the music and make a brief explanation of what he intended to do, the stunt would appeal more to the audience.

At the next show Will walked out and held up his hand. "Stop that noise," he said. The audience roared with delight. Will Rogers had made his first wisecrack from the stage.

"Folks," the cowboy continued, "you can see I got one of these ropes in each hand. When the hoss and rider come out, I'm going to try to throw one of 'em over the hoss and the other over the rider."

Again the audience burst into laughter. Will was angry. He had not meant to say anything comic.

"They laughed at me," he declared as other players assured him he had made a hit.

"Sure, they laughed," the actors replied. "You were funny."

"Funny? Say, I can speak English as good as those folks out there. No, no, I'll never open my mouth again."

For five years "Will Rogers and Company" played in vaudeville for comparatively meager salaries. The "and company" consisted of Buck McKee, horseman, and Teddy, the white horse.

"Sometimes Bill used to make wisecracks at me as I stood in the wings," Buck said, "and often they were heard by those in the first two or three rows of the orchestra. They always laughed and I tried to get Bill to talk louder, but he was bashful.

"One day a theater manager, wondering what was going on, stood beside me and he got a lot of laughs, too. 'Why don't you put that out to the audience?' he asked. Rogers, thinking he meant the roping loop he was spinning out over the audience, explained it was the longest rope he had but he'd try it sometime."

THE QUIP THAT FAILED

But once a wisecrack made by Will was misunderstood by the audience. It happened during his early vaudeville days when he was booked to play in a London music hall. During the act, Rogers ventured some remark about the English having tea in mid-afternoon. The audience thought he was profaning one of their almost sacred customs and hissed and booed. Will retired in confusion.

A short time later in the "lift" in his hotel, Rogers met a fellow American and greeted him: "Howdy. You're from the States?"

The stranger replied: "Yes. I saw your act this afternoon at the music hall."

"It was pretty awful, wasn't it?" replied Will. "I didn't know I was ropin' one of their sacred cows. They can have all the tea they want without me buttin' in again."

That incident may have been the father of the joke that Rogers used to tell of his vaudeville days:

"I did the ropin' and Buck McKee rode our trained, trick pony, Teddy. He was a trick pony because he could do on slippery floors what other ponies did on the range. That was because we had rubber galoshes built for his hoofs.

"Buck used to say he was the lucky one in the act because if the audience got after us, he had a horse to get away on. So I said to Buck: 'If the audience ever gets at us, I'll give you and Teddy half a mile start and pass you. Teddy's boots is to help him stop fast. Mine is built to help me go fast."

"ON BIG TIME"

It was in 1912 that Will Rogers first definitely put his individuality over on a Broadway audience. That year he was one of six cowboys in an act at the Victoria. He had been talking off and on during his wanderings in vaudeville but this was the first time that a "big-time" audience appreciated the significance of his drawling humor. This particular evening, Will missed lassoing the pony as it came galloping across the stage.

"Wal," he drawled, "if he'd a' stuck out his tongue, I'd sho' enough caught him."

The response was spontaneous and uproarious. The Oklahoma drawl registered and the grinning, homely cowboy had come into his own.

When the next season opened, Will Rogers was doing a "single" without the galloping pony and rider. His monolog lasted forty-five minutes in contrast to the ordinary vaudeville turn which was not allowed to run beyond twelve minutes. He kept his audience roaring with his sallies, anecdotes, and shrewd, homely philosophy. He was so good from the beginning on "big-time" that many thought he was just a smart, clever actor who had created a great character rôle.

One of his favorite stunts in those days was to burlesque the act of the famous headliner, Anna Eva Fay, who enjoyed wide reputation as a mind reader. Rogers generally followed her on the bill and her mind readings furnished him with splendid material for good-natured fun. Will would pick out celebrities in the audience and proceed informally to tell their fortunes. Sunday night was the big night for vaudeville at Hammerstein's because all the legitimate theaters were closed. All the satellites of Broadway's night life would be sure to be there. Among them would be "Diamond Jim" Brady, Lillian Russell, Jess Lewisohn, Edna McCauley, Dick Canfield, Tod Sloan, Julia Sanderson, the Schenck Brothers and hosts of other widely known night-lights.

"MIND READING"

Rogers did not know any of these at that time but with the unerring sense of showmanship that was his, he procured their names before the show from a friendly ticket speculator who had sold the celebrities their choice tickets at a heavy premium.

For an hour before he went on the stage, Rogers would question stagehands, managers, friends, and other actors about the persons whose names he had. On the stage, he would mystify and often confound these persons by mentioning where they had been the night before, what ladies the bachelors were paying attention to at the time, how much they had won or lost at the track and card table. As he recited this gossip, he would have a spotlight thrown on the notable he was discussing. Occasionally he would have the spotlight fall on some celebrity only to pass him by without a word of comment. It was done for a joke, but there was no more uncomfortable person along Broadway than the expectant one for whom Rogers had no comment. This always produced as much of a laugh as if he had retailed a choice bit of gossip.

In those old vaudeville days, Rogers used to glance over to the New Amsterdam Theater, where Florenz Ziegfeld was just beginning to make his name in the theatrical world as the producer of beauty and talent. Rogers was walking along Forty-second Street with a friend one night and as they passed the Amsterdam, the friend remarked:

"One of these days your name will be up on that marquee in lights of 100-candle power each."

"Quit kiddin'," retorted Rogers. "There's ten letters in my name and that would take 1,000 candle power. There ain't that much candle power in the whole doggone State of Oklahoma."

Ziegfeld's scouts, always on the lookout for new talent, suggested that the entrepreneur procure Rogers for the Follies, but Ziegfeld only laughed at the thought. At that time Leon Errol and George White were producing the dances, Nora Bayes and Grace Larue were the singing stars, and Kay Laurell, the toast of Broadway, was Ziegfeld's "Little Venus." Miss Laurell later married Winfield Sheehan, who was to become Rogers' guiding genius in the talking motion pictures. The scouts persisted that Rogers would "go great" in the Follies, and Ziegfeld signed him on. It was the beginning of a great friendship and Rogers remained with Ziegfeld from 1914 to 1924, except for a brief period when Will went into the silent movies. Rogers never signed a contract with Ziegfeld or with anyone else on Broadway.

"My word is good," Will said, "and the other feller's ought to be, too."

An example of Rogers' spontaneity was based on his long career with the Follies. Following a polo game at Santa Monica, a fellow player admired Will's physique as he prepared to take a shower.

"Boy," said the player, "you've sure got a great pair of legs on you."

Rogers' blue eyes twinkled and with a roguish grin he replied:

"Why do you think Ziegfeld kept me in the Follies all those years?"

BROADWAY STAR

Will Rogers starred in both the Follies and Ziegfeld's Midnight Frolics on the roof of the New Amsterdam Theater. In that small roof garden, Rogers said he did some of the hardest work of his life. That was due to the fact that the clientele of the roof was made up of a relatively small group that came back night after night. Rogers, in consequence, changed his routine almost nightly. The changing of his monolog also had the effect of making the "repeaters" want to come back nightly to hear his latest quips. There was one quality about Rogers that no comedian of the stage was ever able to equal and that was the fact that he never repeated a gag. While others told and retold the same stories, Will made up new ones as he went along. Some were "pretty sour," as he expressed it, but the bulk of them were "pretty good."

When he was away from New York, Ziegfeld had a habit of firing telegrams at his stars. Will received scores of them but paid no attention to them. At one time, Ziegfeld bombarded Rogers with a bunch of telegrams but the Oklahoman did not answer any of them. The telegrams increased in length and warmth of language. Rogers stopped them by sending the following wire—collect:

"Keep this up. Am on my way to buy more Western Union stock."

FRIENDSHIP FOR "ZIGGY"

When Ziegfeld was dying, it was reported that he was on an obscure ranch in Arizona fighting to

Will Rogers showing his prowess at twirling the lariat during the "Old Spanish Days" at Santa Barbara.

Will Rogers in the first Ziegfeld Follies

regain his health.   The great producer, however, was not in Arizona but in California on the Rogers ranch in the Santa Monica Canyon.   There the best physicians attended him and everything was provided for his recovery and comfort.   Ziegfeld was surrounded with every luxury to which he had become accustomed in his palmiest days.   Rogers saw that he had everything that money could procure and as he expressed it:

"Ziggy gave me my start.   If there is anything I can do to repay him, nothing could be too much."

When Billie Burke, one of the most famous actresses of her time and the widow of Florenz Ziegfeld, heard of Rogers' death in the Arctic, she cried out, "I have lost the best friend a woman ever had."

In his years with the Follies, Will Rogers became a sort of father confessor to that gathering of the world's most beautiful girls.   He watched over them as a father and saved many of them from making a misstep by his homely counsel.   He never sought the position in which the youngsters of the stage placed him, yet they all but worshiped him.   Will had a theory that smoking cigarettes spoiled a woman's beauty, and he passed out packages of chewing gum, which he bought by the gross, to keep the pretty showgirls from using tobacco.

He had a close companionship with his own lovely daughter, Mary, in those days, and once close friends approached him to dissuade her from choosing the theater as a career.   He declined to interfere.

"The more decent women the stage can get, the better it will be for the stage," Will replied.

THAT CHEWING GUM

While Will chewed gum on the stage and advocated it for chorus girls in place of cigarettes, he never chewed it in private life. Rubber bands were his specialty when he wanted to "chaw" upon something offstage. A funny story is told of the vaudeville that played in opposition to Hammerstein's when Will was on the way up. The opposition decided to put on a "cowboy philosopher act" and a number of rope twirlers were rounded up. They were supplied with gags and pushed out on the stage to do their stuff. All of them failed dismally.

"You know the reason," Rogers explained later. "They went out there and chawed tobacco instead of gum."

Will Rogers did not always play the cowboy in leather chaps and Stetson hat. In one of the Follies he essayed a "feminine" rôle in a burlesque of Lenore Ulric, who was starring in *Kiki*. The sketch was entitled *Koo Koo Nell*.

Speaking of that part, Will declared:

"And if I don't go koo-koo myself some night, it will only be because of the triumph of mind over matter. Those darned skirts are getting in my way all the time.

"I have worn the heaviest kind of chaps without difficulty; I have tramped for miles wearing a big old-fashioned overcoat made of buffalo fur, and I have played all kinds of engagements under the greatest difficulties, but I never knew what real trouble was until I tried to act in skirts. You see, the darned old things get in my way in such a manner

that I forget my lines. I never did claim to be much
of an actor, anyhow."

WEARING SKIRTS

"My little old act with the lasso was just put in
to kill time while the girls were changing their
costumes. A male actor's monolog in a girl show is
just like an intermission. So I tried to make my
act attractive by telling a few jokes, and the
audiences laugh, and so Mr. Ziegfeld calls me a star.

"Telling jokes was all right, but when Ned
Wayburn came to me a few weeks ago and said,
'Bill, I'm adding a little dramatic sketch to the
Follies and want you to act one of the rôles,' I
said, 'Well, if this guy isn't kidding me, I haven't
anything to lose because I've got no reputation as
an actor, and if I can make a hit, the critics will
come out and say I am versatile and what not.'
You know what makes a critic—two seats on the
aisle—but I kinder calculated I could make these
critics sit up when I came before them to do a John
Barrymore. But then the blow fell.

"At the first rehearsal I learned they wanted me
to wear skirts.

"Now, skirts is all right in their proper places.
Girls wear them, and sometimes the shortest ones
are worn by old ladies. College boys wear them
when they indulge in amateur theatricals. But to
ask a he-man of the wild and woolly West to wear
skirts in a burlesque show kinder flopped me. I
thought Wayburn was kidding me, and so, to kid
him back, I said, 'Yes.'

"But the darned fool meant it.   He was in earnest.
He brought out the manuscript of *Koo Koo Nell*
and gave me the title rôle.   When I saw I was
really expected to play a girl's rôle and wear skirts,
say, the howling of a prairie dog at midnight was
deep silence to what I said.   But Wayburn insisted;
said I had agreed in front of the whole company to
play the rôle and that my contract with Ziegfeld called
me to play any rôle for which I was cast.   I was roped,
tied, and thrown—and that's how I got into skirts.

"Since I had to wear the blamed things, I decided
to make up as near like Lenore Ulric as *Kiki* as I
possibly could, so I saw that little actress at a
Thursday matinee and ordered my costume built
just like her first-act dress.   The audience gets the
idea of the burlesque at once, especially since
Brandon Tynan as David Belasco is supposed to be
rehearsing the act.   I really tried at first to imitate
Miss Ulric's voice, but no one could quite do that,
so I imitated her mincing ways and cute little business with the powder puff, and, when I went on the
first time, I thought the audience would throw things
at me, but instead they howled.   I didn't know
whether they were laughing with me or agin me, but
so long as they laughed and didn't throw things,
I had no kick coming.

"Now, after playing the darn fool rôle, I am getting used to the skirts and the corset and the plumes
on the hat, and am able to speak my lines without
getting rattled.   I am now studying the rôle of
Ophelia, and hope to play Juliet next season, when
all the other actresses have retired from the combat.

Or, if Miss Ulric ever gets tired of playing *Kiki*, I am willing to take her place if the public will let me. Meanwhile I will keep on throwing the rope and telling my little jokes in the Ziegfeld Follies, unless someone sends me poisoned candy for playing Koo Koo Nell in our little burlesque. It all goes to show that a real actor must be versatile. I never knew I was a real actor before, but it don't pay to quarrel with the critics, and since some of them called me an actor, I'm beginning to believe I am."

FIRST HIT IN THE FOLLIES

Rogers won his way into Ziegfeld's heart the first time he appeared in the Follies in 1914. The World War was raging in Europe and there was no thought at the moment that the United States would ultimately become involved. Henry Ford, the automobile magnate, was planning to send a peace ship abroad with the intention of ending the war by Christmas, or as Ford expressed it, "to take the boys out of the trenches." Twirling his lariat, Rogers let this one fly at the audience:

"Ford's all wrong. Instead of taking along a lot of those high-powered fellers on his ship, he should've hired away all these here Follies' pippins from Flo Ziegfeld. He'd not only get the boys out of the trenches but he'd have Kaiser Bill and Lloyd George and Clemenceau shooting craps to see which one'd head the line at the stage door."

That wisecrack is believed to be the first that Will Rogers ever made upon international affairs. Certainly it is the first that was recorded as such.

Eddie Cantor, blackface comedian, who made his first big hit in the Follies in 1917, recalls that on his opening night when he had gone over in a big way, he broke down and cried in his dressing room. He was feeling sorry that his grandmother, who had encouraged him when the days were blackest and who had died only a few weeks before, could not be present after their years of struggle.

Will Rogers entered the dressing room and Eddie told him why he felt so badly on the biggest night in his career.

"Why, kid," said Rogers, "this is your big night. You're made. Take it big. Smile the tears away. After all, you're an actor. You know what's expected of you."

Five years later Will Rogers telegraphed from California that he would like to be the toastmaster at a dinner given in honor of Cantor by the Friars, a noted club in New York City. At the function he described Eddie Cantor as his "favorite Heeb" and then went on to relate the story of Eddie's first big success.

MEETS PRINCE OF WALES

In 1924, when the Prince of Wales was in America, Will Rogers was among those invited to meet him. On his departure the Prince sold a string of polo ponies he had brought to this country and Will bought one for Patricia Burke Ziegfeld, daughter of his boss, but Ziegfeld supplied the money, according to Rogers. Writing of the incident, the cowboy comedian said:

"It was reported in the press that I purchased one of his ponies for $2,100. Now, that was a mistake. I bought one, but it was for Mr. Flo Ziegfeld's little daughter, and it was him that paid for it. I have some alleged polo ponies of my own; in fact, I think I have the best string of $40 polo ponies in the world, so you would hardly get me giving $2,100 for some old pony just because he belonged to the Prince. I wouldn't give $2,100 for the crown, much less a horse. But, anyway, he was a very nice, gentle, real kid's pony, and little Patricia Burke Ziegfeld was tickled to death with him.

"She had him following her all around, even into the house, and that made a big hit with Mr. Ziegfeld, so he told me: 'What do you know about that pony? Why, Patricia brought him right into the house.'

"I told him, 'Why, after the barns that pony has been used to while he belonged to the Prince of Wales, you were lucky to get him to go into your house. The pony must have thought he was slumming.'

"That's the reason I did not get one. I knew I could not support one in the manner in which it had been accustomed. By the way, the night after the sale, I met the Prince over at a party given in New York by Mrs. Rumsey, and he come over and thanked me for buying the pony, and commenced to tell me what a nice pony it was and all about it. Well, I didn't have the nerve to tell him I had bought the pony for someone else. Incidentally, he asked me if I was not going to tell them some more jokes about him there that night. So I did tell all about the sale and that now that the Prince had sold his ponies, why he could leave. That I thought that was all the British come over for; it was not to play polo, but to sell horses. Incidentally, there was a mix-up in where the check was to be sent to, and that was what delayed his departure for a day. He had not received the money for the pony I bought. Maybe if I had not paid him at all, England never would have got their Prince back."

LOVED TO SING

Will loved to sing but his high tenor voice was better suited for the lonesome reaches of the prairie than the theater. In one show of the Follies the stage manager thought to have some fun with the Oklahoman and told him they had a song for him. Instead of refusing the part as had been anticipated, he accepted gladly and went into rehearsal with it. Ziegfeld was convinced that the singing was the worst he ever heard and ordered it stricken from the show, but Rogers insisted that it be kept in. With a great deal of misgiving, the song was allowed to remain in the show but everyone was confident that it would ruin Rogers' reputation. On the opening night, Will sang the song and the audience nearly rolled in the aisles from laughing. Rogers, it should be explained, knew as Ziegfeld and the others that he couldn't sing, but he did know it would be good show business. It was just another demonstration that above everything else Rogers was a superb showman.

Will Rogers had abandoned the stage for the talking pictures when his close friend, Fred Stone, crashed in an airplane in Connecticut and broke both ankles just before he was to appear as the star in the musical comedy *Three Cheers*. It appeared as if the show could not be put on and the large company that had labored for weeks in rehearsal would get nothing for their pains.

Will dropped all his plans and chartered an airplane for New York. After one day's rehearsal, Rogers stepped into Stone's part, and the show went on. It was a tremendous hit and not only added to Rogers' fame but also introduced Stone's pretty daughter, Dorothy, to stardom.

Charles Dillingham, producer of *Three Cheers*, paid Rogers with a blank check each week, which the comedian filled out himself. No one ever learned the amount that Will took for himself. Whatever the salary was, it did not make up for the financial sacrifice that Rogers made to help out one of his best friends. To take Stone's part until the latter was able to get back on his feet, Rogers canceled movie contracts that would have netted him close to $500,000.

FRIENDSHIP WITH FRED STONE

The friendship between Will Rogers and Fred Stone began outside the stage door of the Knickerbocker Theater in 1906 when Stone and his partner, Dave Montgomery, were costarring in the musical comedy, *The Red Mill.* That famous pair of comedians were rehearsing a new play, entitled *The Old Town,* which was to open at the Globe Theater. Stone planned to do some roping tricks in the show and hired an Indian named Black Chambers to instruct him in the art. One day after a hard rehearsal, Fred Stone was sitting on a bench in the theater alley when a shy young man with an unruly thatch of hair and twinkling blue eyes came up and asked for Fred Stone. Stone arose from the bench and introduced himself. Will explained that he had heard that Chambers, who came from Claremore, Oklahoma, was teaching Stone roping tricks and that he wanted to greet his fellow townsman. Stone told Rogers that Chambers was taken ill and it became necessary to send the young Indian back to Oklahoma.

"I am a roper," Rogers told Stone. "What are you doin'? Learnin' trick ropin'?"

Stone replied that all he wanted to learn was to spin a rope while dancing inside the swirling loop.

"Shucks," replied Rogers, "I'll teach you all the ropin' you want to know."

The two went inside the theater, and Rogers gave Stone a demonstration of handling a lariat as only a master could do it. That was the beginning of one of the finest friendships in the theater, and it grew with the years. Stone readily picked up the rope-spinning trick and used it for many years as a part of his routine in musical comedy.

Will gave this testimonial of his friendship for the nimble-footed and versatile Stone, who was one of the greatest luminaries of his day:

"When I agree to sing, that's the greatest evidence of sincere friendship I could show," Rogers declared.

Rogers also learned to dance, but none of the thousands that paid to see and hear him, however, gave up their money to see him trip the light fantastic or hear him warble one of the popular ballads. They paid toll to listen to his latest jest.

"It wouldn't be my luck for your father to be a dramatic actor," Rogers used to say to Dorothy Stone. "He had to be a dancer. That's tough, because I would like to take a crack at that Barrymore stuff. I know I could ruin a good drama."

"I hadda take dancing lessons for this show," he would tell the audience. "Taking up dancing at my age is like taking up golf at your age, but if I must say so, some of my dancing is just as good as some of your golf."

SUBSTITUTED OWN LINES

When Rogers joined *Three Cheers,* the producers were smart enough to allow Rogers to substitute his own lines whenever he saw fit. No one else but Will could have conceived them, and their freshness and originality was evidenced by the fact that often the cast had to stop and laugh themselves.

In Stone's show, Rogers made a lot of fun out of an operation he had undergone a short time before. He described how he entered the hospital and how one nurse after another came in, punctured the end of his finger with a bodkin to take samples of his blood. When the fifth blood pirate appeared in the room, Rogers waved her away and declared:

"No more blood here. I believe you girls are keeping a friend who is anemic."

A diagnostician, he explained in connection with his operation, was a traffic cop for physicians who directed patients to left-leg doctors when they really should be sent to right-leg specialists.

Will's "ad libbing" in the show forced the other players to be constantly on their guard. Andy Tombes, who himself was one of the great comics of the stage, avoided difficulty by learning Rogers' part as written by the authors. Incidentally, despite Rogers' joke about singing, members of the cast declared that the part Will enjoyed most was the place where he was called upon to sing a duet with Tombes.

While Will Rogers was with the Follies before he became the featured star, the other luminaries on the bill frequently complained about the size of type in which their names were displayed. After a rumpus over this point, one manager told Ziegfeld that he would never "book" the Follies for his theater again. Ziegfeld then declared he would cut all billing for stars and merely advertise the Follies. He broke this rule only for Rogers, and the cowboy philosopher was "billed ahead" of the show in this fashion:

WILL ROGERS
in Ziegfeld Follies

When Rogers first abandoned the stage for the moving pictures, Florenz Ziegfeld warned him to "watch out for those movie cuties."

"Shucks," replied Will, "if your gals couldn't break me down in all these years, what chance has those in the movies got?"

CHAPTER V

ROGERS IN THE MOVING PICTURES

WILL ROGERS was a stage star of the first magnitude when Samuel Goldwyn, the producer, persuaded him to quit Broadway to go into the moving pictures in 1919. The plays were far from being startling successes, but Goldwyn, with that uncanny sense of showmanship that boosted him to the top, realized that as a movie actor Rogers possessed a homely quality that would appeal to the masses. Goldwyn was ahead of his time, for the silent films could not reproduce the inimitable drawl with its multitude of inflections. To star in the movies at that time, the actor had to captivate the younger generation by his looks, and the cowboy philosopher, who looked as if he had just finished cutting his own hair with a pair of dull sheepshears, could not display his great personality to the best advantage.

EARLY DAYS IN THE MOVIES

Rogers was asked in those early days how he happened to enter the films and he replied:

"When Goldwyn decided to make fewer and worse pictures, he sent for me."

It was Rex Beach, brother-in-law of Fred Stone, who introduced Rogers to Goldwyn. Beach told the picture producer that Will was the man to play the part of Bill Hyde, hero of Beach's novel, which was being adapted for the screen by Goldwyn. On the screen the picture became *Laughing Bill Hyde,* and Rogers played the title rôle.

Rogers' own version of how he was approached on the subject of entering the moving pictures is a masterpiece of wit.

"I've knocked around all over the world," he said. "I was born in the old Indian Territory and I grew up on a cow pony but I prefer to travel in a Pullman. I can shoot pretty straight but I've got no notches on my gun. I never even shot up an ice-cream parlor or a cigar store. Most of the Wild West stuff is pulled off in the big cities, anyway.

"I didn't have any more intention of going into pictures than I had of being president of Yale. I was living quiet and peaceful down in Amityville, Long Island, where the insane asylum is, when Mrs. Rex Beach came driving down there one day.

"She steps out of her royalty on *The Spoilers* and says: 'Will, you're goin' into the movies.'

"I pointed over to the place where they kept the lunatics and told her chauffeur he had come to the wrong place.

" 'No, Will, I'm serious,' Mrs. Beach says.

"I told her my hair wasn't curly, that I couldn't roll a cigarette with one hand, and that I didn't aim to annoy more than one audience at a time.

" 'You've got to come, Will,' she insisted. 'The movies is the third biggest business in the world. Safety razors is first, corn plasters second, and movies third.'

"Well, in I went. Since then the movies has become the second biggest business in the country. Bootlegging is the biggest. The movies is the grandest show business I know anything about. It's the only place where an actor can act and at the same time sit down in front and clap for himself."

Rogers told Goldwyn that he couldn't act, and when the producer offered him a contract, he replied: "You're waving that paper at the wrong boy, Mr. Goldwyn. Why, if I was to take up your proposition, you'd be the maddest man in the world before you got through with me."

Laughing Bill Hyde was produced at the Goldwyn studio in Fort Lee, New Jersey, and the picture made money for the producer, but nothing like the fabulous sums that were to pour into the coffers of the Fox Company when Rogers appeared in the talking pictures.

After the first picture was finished, Goldwyn took Rogers to see it one day and said: "Now, what do you say, Mr. Rogers? Are you an actor?"

"Yep," replied Rogers. "You're right, I'm an actor, all right. The worst in the world. My answer is still the same. Leave the acting business to them that can act. All I know how to do is to throw a lariat and crack jokes."

Rogers' estimate of himself was always modest in the extreme. He frequently told fellow actors that he could not act and the only time he was any good was "when they found a part that's sorta like me." "He expressed a similar opinion of his skill with the lariat: "I'm the poorest roper in the world."

But that was Rogers. As an actor, he essayed many rôles and performed them with a rare skill that others could not imitate. As a roper, he was one of the best that ever appeared on the stage.

In 1920, Rogers made *Jubilo*, and Goldwyn always was of the opinion that this film was the Oklahoman's greatest achievement in silent pictures. It was a melodrama, in which Rogers played the part of a forlorn, old tramp. Motion-picture critics of that period accorded the film only casual notice, and the same was true of other films of that day. Regardless of the opinion of the critics, Goldwyn continued to star Rogers in the silent films. They must have made him some money by proving popular with the movie fans of the day, for no producer would have featured a player in one film after another unless he brought in the box-office receipts.

Among the silent pictures in which Rogers starred were: *Almost a Husband; Honest Hutch; Jes' Call Me Jim; Two Wagons, Both Covered; Doubling For Romeo; Boys Will Be Boys; Family Fits; Our Congressman; The Headless Horseman; Going to Congress; Gee Whiz; Genevieve;* and *A Texas Steer.*

In those early days on the movie lot, an assistant director told Rogers that he would have to ride a horse in one of the scenes. The assistant then went on to explain that if he couldn't ride, a "double" would be provided for him. Will looked at the young man quizzically and asked:

"Where's the horse?"

On being shown the animal, Rogers leaped upon his back and cut across the lot in good, old cowboy fashion. The assistant director, who had made the mistake of thinking that Will was strictly a "Broadway cowboy," stood open-mouthed as Rogers put the horse through his paces.

WRITES HIS OWN TITLES

In a film travelog, entitled *In Paris,* in which Rogers appeared in those days, the titles were written by him. Without the picture, the effect of many of them was lost, but some of the others are amusing by themselves. They were:

"Well, folks, here we-all are in 'Gay Paree,' but 'count of the French custom of throwing rocks at American tourists I'm going to disguise myself as a 'Frog.' " [Will then put on a small, pointed, black mustache.]

"Now if you sightseers will all keep still and don't start braggin' about where you come from, they'll never know we're Americans."

"Come on, folks, crawl into the Limberneck hack and I'll show you the Claremore, Oklahoma, of France."

"First, I'll show you the most thrilling spot in Paris—the place where Americans go every day to see if their friends back home have cabled the money."

"Here's the French Opera. If this was in America, if would be a movie house."

"This chateau on the right is the Café de la Paix [pay]—and if you are an American, you will."

"These saloons are so full, half the people can't get in—so they set them on the sidewalk."

"Le Grand Boulevard! Translated into Oklahoma English it means 'Main Stem.'"

"Here's the Eiffel Tower. Charley Schwab sold them the steel, Otis put in the elevators, and the Americans go up and look. It's a traffic tower for angels and airplanes."

"They call this the Latin Quarter, because no one speaks Latin and no one has a quarter."

"These are the Tuileries, the world's most beautiful gardens. That thing spouting out is a fountain. If a thing was spouting at home, it would be a Senator."

"The French have done very well with their art when you consider they use only two subjects—the nude woman and the lion. And even the lion is nude."

"This is the Louvre, France's great picture gallery. It's the nearest thing France has to our Hollywood. The Louvre has more art but Hollywood has more excitement."

"Let me present Mona Lisa, the only beauty who went through history and retained her reputation."

RETURN TO THE STAGE

After three years before the camera, Rogers became convinced that the stage offered him the best medium of expression, and he returned to the New Amsterdam roof, where he opened his new act in a masked dance in which he impersonated a showgirl of the Ziegfeld Frolic. Will wore a pair of pink satin slippers and a cape in his impersonation but he presented the act only once in public.

"I wore the pink satin slippers just once and that was enough," Rogers said. "Besides, I think it was silly, even if people did laugh when I threw off my cloak."

To fellow actors, Will confessed that he was glad to get away from the movie lots and return to the theater.

"It's a great thing," he said, "to get the old brain workin' again after loafing on the movie lots. You know, you've got to exercise your brain just like your muscles. I found when I went back, that I wasn't as good as I used to be. I was all out of practice."

FIRST "TALKIE"

When sound projection proved successful, Winfield R. Sheehan, then executive head of the Fox Films sought his bosom friend, Will Rogers, and persuaded him to return to take a chance on the "talkies."

"Aw, Winnie," protested Will, "I'll probably mess your picture all up."

But Sheehan was of a different opinion, and Rogers went to Hollywood to make *They Had To See Paris*, which was produced in 1929. The picture registered as a smash hit throughout the country and immediately established Rogers as the leading box-office attraction. Fox made about $700,000 profit on the picture, and Will's contract called for the production of another picture immediately. Before it was started, however, Fred Stone cracked up in his airplane. Rogers chartered an airplane and flew to New York to take his friend's part so that the show

might go on. Aside from his great friendship for
Stone, it was said that Rogers was motivated by the
thought that more than 100 persons, actors, showgirls, and stage artisans, would be thrown out of
work unless the show went on. *Three Cheers* had
a long run, and then one day Will Rogers faced the
difficult task of playing Fred Stone, while the
veteran comedian was in the audience. Late in
1930, Rogers went back to Hollywood.

The first picture he made on his return to Hollywood was *So This Is London*, and one of the uproarious bits occurs when Rogers is playing the rôle of
a seasick passenger crossing the Atlantic Ocean.
He was wrapped in blankets and seated in a steamer
chair when a dizzy young thing noticed his misery
and inquired airily, "Is this your first crossing?"

Rogers looked up at her wanly from the depths
of his coverings and replied, "Does anyone ever go
again?"

IN FAMOUS RÔLES

His next appearance on the talking screen was in
the rôle of Bill in *Lightnin'*, the character made
famous by Frank Bacon on the legitimate stage.
As Bill Jones, the lovable old inventor, Rogers had
a part that in many ways was like himself. Bill,
however, was a shiftless husband, and by no stretch
of the imagination could Will Rogers have been
found guilty on that score in real life even in the
smallest degree.

In the *Connecticut Yankee*, a modernization and
adaptation of Mark Twain's famous tale, *A Connecticut*

Yankee in King Arthur's Court, Rogers was a radio engineer who was transported back to the days of Knights of the Round Table after being stunned by an electrical outburst in a gigantic and mysterious radio set.   In Mark Twain's original version, the first Yankee was carried back to King Arthur's time after being hit over the head in a fight with a fellow worker.   In the filming of the picture, the question arose whether Will Rogers could be induced to wear tights.   It was said that he objected in the beginning and in the early scenes he wore his conventional blue overalls.   Even in the jousting scene when he might have been expected to appear like other knights, he insisted upon a costume of his own design and it did not include tights.   Near the end of the picture when Will donned armor to go out and rescue the pretty princess from the wicked queen, he capitulated. When his captors denuded him of his iron shirt and pants, Rogers stood clad in tights.

In the picture *Young as You Feel,* Rogers showed that he could not only wear clothes as well as any other great actor but that he could play parts that were decidedly unlike himself in real life.   Appearing first as a groaning dyspeptic who set the time by the punctuality with which he takes his pills, Rogers, as Lemuel Morehouse, throws off the cloak of illness and appears attired in the height of fashion.   A checkered suit with a pearl-gray waistcoat, derby and spats to match, all designed for the racetrack, showed that Rogers got as much fun out of wearing fancy clothes as did his audiences at seeing him arrayed in all his glory.   Will overcame his reputed

aversion to evening dress and appeared in a fault-
lessly cut suit and a silk topper. All this went to
prove that Will Rogers was a superb showman, who
clung to his careless manner of dress because it was
his trade-mark and the finest kind of show business.

In *Business and Pleasure*, Rogers was again called
upon to play the part of a business man, while in the
play *Ambassador Bill* he was a politician. Although
there was nothing that savored of the Wild West,
he was allowed to be just Will Rogers in the picture
Happy Days. He was a plutocratic business man
in *Down to Earth* but in his next vehicle, *Too Busy
to Work*, he was a happy, go-lucky tramp. Next
he played the rôle of a farmer who specialized in
hog raising in *State Fair*, and in *Doctor Bill* he was a
country doctor. Will was the proprietor of a "fixit"
shop in *Mr. Skitch*, and in *David Harum* he was a
banker and horse trader.

AN ACTOR OF RARE TALENT

Rogers, despite all his fun making, was an emotional actor of rare talent. It used to be one of the
favorite and moss-covered jokes of the stage that
the low comedian always aspired to the rôle of the
Melancholy Dane. Rogers proved that it takes a
great comedian to play an emotional part. During
the filming of *Judge Priest* he played the leading
part in *Ah, Wilderness* on the stage and when the
show opened in San Francisco, he was accorded one
of the greatest ovations ever given a star in that
city. His performance of the sympathetic rôle,
created by that other great comedian, George M.

Cohan, was acclaimed by dramatic critics as one of the outstanding triumphs of the stage. Rogers said that after all his years of comedy he essayed the rôle in *Ah, Wilderness* as a personal experiment and he really felt that he might be a "notable flop."

Frank Borzage, who directed Will Rogers in *They Had To See Paris* and *Young as You Feel*, expressed the idea very clearly:

"The one thing that made Will Rogers the outstanding comedian in the films was his own ability to make audiences forget that he was a comedian. This quality of his was very apparent in the scenes where Rogers was called upon to portray the simple, human emotions that touch the very soul of mankind. The sincerity and conviction with which he did them is what might be expected of a great tragedian. Audiences forget Rogers as a wisecracker and think of him only as a human being torn with emotion."

Rogers' death in the Arctic cut short a production schedule of ten proposed pictures for the Fox Company. The humorist had signed to appear in ten pictures, at a salary of $200,000 each, and had completed three of them. The three completed pictures were *Steamboat Round the Bend, Doubting Thomas,* both released shortly before the tragedy, and *In Old Kentucky.*

There was some question raised about the propriety of releasing Rogers' pictures after his death. David Butler, motion-picture director, who knew Will as the working man better probably than any other person, told how the humorist once answered this question. Rogers was deeply affected by the deaths of Knute Rockne, football coach at the University of Notre Dame, and Marie Dressler, the film star.

"'You know, Dave,' Butler recalled Rogers as having said when they were talking about Miss Dressler, 'there is a permanent record of her on these talking pictures, and she'll always be with us. Don't worry, old Will himself will always be there, too, unless they get tired of me.'

DRESSING ROOM A RUMBLE SEAT

"Will's dressing room was the rumble seat of his car, and many times he would come tearing up to the stage in his car or on location where we were working. If he'd be late, he'd yell, 'Hold on there, boys, I'm coming.' He'd jump out of the car, dash around to the back, and don his pants and shirt and in a second he would be ready for work.

"He would never sleep in his dressing room as the other stars did. He'd hitch those old spectacles on the end of his nose, slide down into a chair, his face hidden in a newspaper, pretending he was reading. But he would be snoozing.

"After a while I would go over and tap him and he would awaken with a jerk, clear his throat, and say, 'Look here, Dave, did you read this story in the paper? Plumb interestin'.'"

Butler declared that Rogers disliked learning the lines as written in the scenario. He would have Butler give him the general theme of the scene and then the humorist would supply many of his own

A scene from *Life Begins at 40*, in which Will Rogers and George Barbier decide to shoot it out, while Richard Cromwell, Jed Prouty, and Thomas Beck look on.

Will Rogers, "The Boss," together with William Farnum and Brandon Hurst, as they appeared in *A Connecticut Yankee*.

Janet Gaynor and **Will Rogers** in *State Fair*

Will Rogers dressed for a screen role in *As Young as You Feel*

lines. Seldom did Rogers ask that the mechanical crew on his set work overtime, but whenever a picture was completed ahead of schedule, the comedian would make up the loss to the men by paying them out of his own pocket.

In all, he made nineteen talking pictures. None of them earned less than one million dollars at the box office and it has been estimated that he brought in more than $25,000,000 to the treasury of the Fox Company while he was in their employ.

On the movie lots in Hollywood, everyone loved Will Rogers and nobody was jealous of him, which was by the way of being a miracle, when the temperament of movie stars was considered. No upstage for Rogers. Never did he demand anything as the highest salaried star in the business. He spent half his time "gabbing" with the five-dollar and ten-dollar-a-day extras. Often they were just a tryout audience for some wisecrack that would appear the next day in his daily writings or as a gag in his pictures.

SCORNED LUXURIOUS DRESSING ROOM

While he talked, he chewed, sometimes gum, but mostly rubber bands or the tips of his spectacles. He claimed that eighteen pairs of spectacles were chewed up every two years. Overalls, high-heeled cowboy boots, and an old sweater was his usual costume about the movie lots. He looked more like a cow hand than the greatest star.

Rogers had the only reserved table in the commissary on the Fox lot. He invariably drank two cups of coffee, regardless of what he ate, and always paid the checks of all those who sat at his table. He scorned a luxurious dressing room. The studio fixed an adobe hut in the midst of a beautiful garden for him to occupy. The place had an electric kitchen and a living room adorned with Western and Indian trophies. Rogers looked in and said: "It is swell," and never went back until President and Mrs. Coolidge visited him. He ushered them into the house and later explained it by saying: "Well, they had to set somewheres, didn't they?"

Every year Henry Ford and Walter Chrysler presented Rogers with a new roadster or coupé and he used it for an office and a dressing room. In the rumble seat he kept twelve ties, two suits of clothes, and a portable typewriter. That was his movie and literary equipment. When he was not working or eating in the company restaurant, he would generally be found seated upon the running board of his automobile with his typewriter on his lap writing "a piece for the papers."

ROGERS' LOVE OF PEOPLE

He was always on time and after he had the action of the scene to be photographed thoroughly in his mind, he would ask what clothes he was to wear. Then he'd go to his car, pick out a tie, or perhaps change his suit. Then he would work until noon when he would call out, "Lunchee!" That was a signal for a dash to the restaurant and he would be the first one there. His love of food was equaled only by his desire to travel and meet people.

Rogers called the restaurant "his club" and often he toured the room, stopping to chat for a moment with stenographers, script girls, extras, and others who earned only modest salaries. After passing the time of day with them, he would pick up their checks and pay for their lunches. When he was out on location, Will took a box lunch along and sat down with the mechanics, carpenters, and extras to eat it.

When he returned to the set after luncheon, Rogers always took a half hour or more to "grind out" his daily newspaper feature. This finished, he would read it to a stage carpenter or a director. If their reaction was good, it would be sent at once to the telegraph office. About 4.30 every afternoon Rogers would begin spinning imaginary ropes as a signal to the director that he was impatient to be off for his Santa Monica ranch to rope a few steers, a pastime of which he never tired.

Once he was playing in a scene in the late afternoon and it was decided to continue it after supper. The action called for Rogers to take the same place as before. The camera was aimed at the back of his head. As they were about to shoot the scene, the director noticed to his horror that Rogers had had his hair cut during the supper hour. The director explained to Rogers that it would be ridiculous to see long hair one minute and short hair the next. The picture was spoiled, he assured Rogers. Will grinned.

"Shucks," he said. "If it's a good picture, they won't notice it and if it's bad, it won't matter."

Rogers had very strict ideas of what he would do for the moving pictures. He wouldn't portray smoking or drinking although he did not mind if other characters did it in his pictures when such action was necessary to the plot. In *Doubting Thomas* Will was supposed to take a cigar from his pocket and hand it to another player. He refused on the ground that he didn't smoke and the action would be unlike him.

Visitors to the Fox movie lots always asked to see Will Rogers first. If those making the request were prominent enough, they were presented to him and during his career in Movietone City he entertained more celebrities than any of the others in Hollywood's royal families. A list of the notables who called upon him would read like a selection of names from the front pages of the newspapers. While he was engaged in filming *Business and Pleasure*, he was visited by Patrick J. Hurley, then Secretary of War, Colonel and Mrs. Charles A. Lindbergh, David Ingalls, Secretary of Aëronautics for the Navy; Helen Wills, the tennis queen; Frank Hawks, the aviator, Florenz Ziegfeld, Prince Svasti of Siam and his royal family, the Four Horsemen of Notre Dame football fame, and scores of others equally well known.

Instead of taking the callers through the plant in his own car, Rogers took great delight in offering them the novelty of the studio's private transportation system. This was a bus with a uniformed driver. Luncheon was sometimes served in his dressing room. It was a mystery to many at the studio how a man who neither drank, smoked, played cards, golf, nor tennis could enjoy his fame as a host.   The secret was in his conversational ability.   Rogers even talked to himself, a habit that probably carried over from his cowboy days on the Oklahoma range. A week-end guest at the Rogers ranch was a three-day show, with Rogers keeping up a running fire of Western, political, Hollywood, and darky stories. One of his unrealized ambitions was to make a picture in blackface.

Rogers' death cut short a proposed production schedule of ten pictures for the Fox Twentieth Century Company.   He had signed to appear in the films until 1938.

Steamboat Round the Bend, which was released just about the time he died, was hailed by critics everywhere as probably his greatest picture.   The character, as always, was Will Rogers, the movie actor, who, in 1934 and 1935, was rated as the player who had drawn the largest number of patrons to the movie houses of the country.   In the picture Will again showed his rare ability of timing his scenes perfectly, of modulating his voice in the exact tone, and of emphasizing the humor with a spontaneity that made it appear as if acting were fun, instead of the hardest kind of work.

Irvin S. Cobb, who played with him in the picture, tells how Rogers magnanimously gave Anne Shirley, the pretty young actress who played the lead, her chance to shine in one of the important scenes.   Cobb, the famous humorist and writer, was induced to play in the picture at the insistence of Rogers. Cobb told how Will drew John Ford, the director, aside during a lull in the play.

"John," Rogers said, "this kid is good—she's swell. And she's such a sweet little thing, off and on. Makes me think of my own Mary, somehow. What say, let her dominate this scene instead of me?"

Ford, according to Cobb, told Rogers that he was the star and Will replied: "I'm gettin' the star's billin' and the star's salary, but the star of this picture, man or woman, is the one that can steal it. Have a heart, John, give the kid a chance."

And John had a heart, Cobb declared.

CHAPTER VI

Rogers on the Radio

THE NEWEST means of entertainment, the radio, was not long in claiming Will Rogers for one of its stellar performers and for his broadcasts over the air. In his radio talks, he found that Presidents made shining targets for his barbed shafts of humor. But in January, 1928, there was a suspicion that he had overstepped the bounds as "court jester of the United States." Rogers was hired to act as master of ceremonies at a radio jubilee. The program proceeded according to schedule with Rogers introducing his old friends, Fred Stone, Al Jolson, Paul Whiteman, and others.

At the end, Rogers announced that he had a surprise. Will was pleased, he said, to present the President of the United States, who would speak on national affairs from the White House. A New England twang, exactly like that of Calvin Coolidge, was heard on the loud speakers.

"It gives me great pleasure to report on the state of the nation," said the voice. "The nation is prosperous on the whole, but how much prosperity is there in a hole?"

Thousands thought it was President Coolidge speaking and the next day protests were made at the White House. Will was downhearted because his prank had been misunderstood, but some days later he announced with obvious relief in his voice that Coolidge had not minded the burlesque in the least.

No other joke he ever made on the radio again was questioned on the grounds of good taste.

Later, Rogers laughed at the Coolidge incident when he met Mrs. Coolidge, and she assured Will that she could have given a better imitation of her husband.

"Well, Grace," replied Will, "you can imitate Cal's voice better'n me, but look what you had to go through to learn it."

$72,000 FOR FIFTEEN MINUTES

In March, 1930, Will signed a contract for fourteen radio talks of fifteen-minute duration and was paid $72,000. Some protested that the sum of about $350 a minute was far too much and that Rogers couldn't possibly be worth that much.

The editors of *World's Work* printed a defense of Will's receiving this vast salary, and pointed out that Rogers' stories were all spontaneous and without prolog. The editors wrote:

"All this is to the good. But there is something more than this about Will Rogers. His chief interest is not in the affairs of foreign potentates, but in the manners and customs of the great American public. Here it seems to be his mission, under the guise of genial raillery, to tell us the hard, blunt truths about ourselves—truths about our politics, our civic standards, and our social habits. They are the sort of truths we do not always like to hear, but we will take them with a contagious chuckle and a piece of chewing gum.

During the filming of his biography of Napoleon, Emil Ludwig was guest of honor at a dinner of the Writers' Club. He is shown with Captain Peter Freuchen, Danish writer, and Will Rogers.

Will Rogers and Irwin S. Cobb, stars in one of Rogers'
last films, *Steamboat Round the Bend*

Shirley Temple, the popular child star, and Will Rogers
were great pals.

"Will Rogers gives them to us in that manner. Confession is good for the soul, and he supplies it. That may be one large reason for his salary."

What was not made public was the fact that Will Rogers never touched a cent of the $72,000. The money was turned over to one of his many charities.

THE FAMOUS ALARM CLOCK

On his first broadcast in a new series of entertainments, Will Rogers put over one of his best gags. What appeared to be an alarm clock sounded as he neared the end of his talk. It was supposed to be a signal that he was to stop "gabbing" and let the rest of the show go on. There was no clock at all. It was an electric bell which Will rang himself and then muttered something about the untimely "interruption."

Rogers refused to let network officials censor his broadcasts and, according to reports, there were frequent tiffs over this point. He even poked fun at the radio on a nation-wide hook-up in November, 1934, when the National Broadcasting Company was celebrating a "birthday party."

"Tonight's anniversary is not so much a testimonial to the work of the radio as it is an example of the perseverance and good will of the American people.

"They tell you it has been a great cementer of good will among countries. I don't suppose there was ever a time in our history when as many nations were just ready to start shooting at each other as there are now.

"Nothing that makes people acquainted makes friends. If somebody invented something where nobody knew anything about anything, that would be really a forward step in world peace.

"You never argue with a woman unless you are married to her. Nations never fight unless they know each other. But what would we do without a radio? At any hour of the day or night, tune in and somebody is telling you how to live, how to vote, how to drink, how to think, when to wash your teeth, when to wash your hair, when to cut your whiskers, when to see your doctor, and how to see your doctor, and when to see your priest, and when to see your preacher, and how to put on fat, and how to take off fat, and how to make the skin stay white and how to make it stay black.

"Honest, no other nation in the world would stand for such advice as that. But we do, and we like it. So the only thing that can make us give up our radio is poverty. The old radio is the last thing moved out of the house when the sheriff comes in.

"It's an invention that has knocked nobody out of work and that gives work to many people. That is something you can't say for many inventions. So, as bad as it is, I don't know, it is the best invention I think that has ever been."

IN MEMORIAM TO KNUTE ROCKNE

In addition to broadcasting on commercial programs, Rogers would go before the microphone for anyone almost who might ask him, provided the cause was a worthy one. When a campaign was in

progress in November, 1931, to raise funds for a
memorial to Knute Rockne, famous Notre Dame
football coach, it would have been almost impossible
to have kept Will from broadcasting, for Rockne was
one of his dearest friends. Rockne, like Rogers,
died in an airplane crash.

There were tears in Rogers' eyes at one point when
he spoke just as if Rockne could hear his voice:

"You would acknowledge the hard times there
are now. You would have told your listeners of the
needs of the unemployed. You would have asked
that we give to them first and to this fund after we
had done our duty to the less fortunate.

"You would not ask, nor would you have taken
any man's last dollar. You would have only asked
the giver to give in proportion to the satisfaction
which the spirit of a great team has given."

A short time before the radio speech, Rogers had
eulogized "Rock" at a luncheon given in memory of
the great coach by the Los Angeles Chamber of
Commerce. Will was not on the program, but the
toastmaster saw him in the room and asked him to
speak. Those in the room declared they would
never forget that day as Rogers unashamedly stood
with tears streaming down his face and for
twenty-five minutes told jokes about Rockne,
sobbed, and then went on tell more jokes.

When he got up to speak, he said:

"It is terrible when a comedian is sad. But after
all, comedy and sentiment are not very far apart.
It's hard that the death of a great man has to give
a luncheon club its only excuse for meeting."

Turning to football and commenting on the high esteem with which Rockne was held, he continued:

"We owe him more than he could know. His last football game was played in Los Angeles last December and it kept us from contracting the worst case of swelled head the world has ever known. He cured us in a business-like fashion when Notre Dame licked Southern California. If he hadn't won that game, we would have thought every boy east of the Mississippi was anemic.

"Rock was the best after-dinner speaker we had. I would have hated to follow him. He told me many stories. I got 'em for nothing, then retold 'em and collected. If there was anybody to whom I owed royalties to, it was Rock."

Rogers told how he had visited South Bend, Indiana, and how he saw little children playing football there.

"Rock said that if a smart coach wanted to know what Notre Dame was doing in secret practice he could watch the children running all the formations just like the varsity. But Rock knew, of course, that there were no smart coaches."

The humorist then recounted how Rockne had taken his team to see Rogers on the stage as a reward for defeating West Point in one of the classic Army-Notre Dame games. Rogers, knowing they were in the audience, procured a Notre Dame sweater with its familiar N.D. monogram and spoke much pride about his "alma mater." After lauding the college and the team to the skies, he concluded with:

"And now. let's all give a cheer for North Dakota."

TRIBUTE TO HERBERT HOOVER

In one of his appeals over the radio for the Red Cross, he paid a stirring tribute to former President Hoover.

"It was good to hear the Revelers," he said. "I want to thank them again. They are the ones that helped Frank Hawks and I when we were on our tour for the drought relief in the South.

"I'm going to talk a little tonight about Mr. Hoover, for Mr. Hoover was originally to appear on this program.

"I think Mr. Hoover is a great man, just as great as he ever was. It hurts no man's reputation not to be able to reorganize politics. Mr. Hoover, it may be small compensation to you, but today you carry more sincere sympathy than any man that has been President during our lifetime, with the possible exception of Mr. Wilson during the war.

"You were very unfortunate. You certainly had a tough break. You just happened to be the man that was left watching the dam when the dam busted and we expected that you would put the water back. Not a soul in America will ever crow to you. They will moan with you, but they won't exult over you.

"You just didn't speak a politican's language. You naturally couldn't get used to having him do everything backwards. It wasn't you personally. They just wanted to trade horses and they would have done so even if you had been riding 'Man o' War.'

"Don't take politics too serious, Mr. Hoover, it is just another American racket. Washington is just a joint and you don't know when it is going to be raided by the opposition gang.

"The machine gun is the ballot box and she is loaded with 'nay' votes. You can be a Senator or a Congressman or a big shot today but tomorrow you are liable to be paying for your own stamps.

MR. HUGHES AND THE RED CROSS

"Now tonight we had Mr. Hughes with us. We have been on charity drives together. One summer in coming home on the boat from Europe together, they played a big benefit for the relief of Florida from the tornado and 10,000 Yankee real-estate men.

"We got $50,000 from the passengers on the *Leviathan* in one night. That was coming this way. When Europe heard there was $50,000 they overlooked from these people, they have been sore at Mr. Hughes and I ever since.

"Mr. Hughes is a great character. You that have never had the good fortune to meet him think that he is all intellect. When you see behind those whiskers, he is a real human man."

"Mr. Hughes, now he was put on this program to make the appeal to you for this best cause we have in our land, the Red Cross. I was simply put on the program for the benefit of those who didn't understand Mr. Hughes's English.

"It has been a pleasure to appear with you, Mr. Hughes. You are the one Republican I know of that needs no consolation on the late catastrophe. You are on the Supreme Bench where the Democrats can't get at you. If they pass a law to throw you

out, you can say the law ain't constitutional. You
got the surest racket there is, Mr. Hughes.

"There are two things we have in our government
that we honor and treasure—that is the Supreme
Court of the United States and the Red Cross of
America.

"We know they will function without fear or favor.
The poorest in our land will always receive justice
from our Supreme Court and the poorest will always
receive the necessities from our American Red
Cross. Thank you."

RADIO EXPLOITATION OF MOTHER'S DAY

The fallacy and sham behind the exploitation of
Mother's Day was exposed by Rogers in one of his
wittiest radio addresses in May, 1935.

He credited the idea of the day to the business
acumen of the florists.

"Of course," he says, "florists—they got mothers,
too . . . florists have, but they got more flowers
than they've got mothers and, and they got a great
selling organization.

"It's nothing unusual any day for me to get a
telegram saying Congressman Jasbo just died. We
have a special spray of beautiful lilies we're holding
until we hear from you. The florists—they've just
practically corraled this Mother's Day business."

He suggests that it might have been better for
Mother had the "meat growers" taken the idea
over first.

"Instead of receiving a bunch of hollyhocks, you
know, she'd receive a cluster of pork chops.

"A mother is the only thing that is so constituted
that they possess eternal love under any and all cir-
cumstances. No matter how you treat them, you
still have the love . . . I was telling that to my wife
today and I said—a mother and a dog is the only
two friends that has eternal love. No matter how
you treat 'em—and my wife makes me cut the dog
out. Said it didn't sound very good, and it might
sound disrespectful to a mother, but I certainly didn't
mean it that way, but it's the only thing that really is.

"And now Mother—you—you know, no matter if
the children don't write to her, that don't never make
no difference. It don't, it don't. Her faith is just
as long as her memory.

"Mothers are naturally glad to have this day
dedicated to 'em and they're glad we pay them this
homage and remembrance but it hasn't increased
their love one bit. It's made no changes in her. She
can see through this Mother's Day thing, you know.
She knows we were almost forced by law to do
something about her and there's no conceit in a
mother."

He proposed a practical substitute for the "flowers
a mother can't eat."

"My plan is to give mothers more than one day.
Pardon my generosity toward mothers. It may be
unfounded, but I'd just give mothers at least twelve
days a year. I'd say, for instance—I'd say every
month is going to be Mother's Day.

"January first we'd start off, and that would be
mother's forgotten Christmas present day. Incidentally, they could send her some present that they

got that they didn't care for, too. Then February first would be gloves and mittens and overshoes day. She'd have worn out the old ones chopping wood to cook for you.

"And then one day would be Mother's Dress Day. Mother hasn't had a new dress since father went to jail for it. They can have that, too.

"Mother's Transportation Day is next. Give her a new automobile. If you can't afford that, a bicycle and a pair of shorts. That would be a great thing for these modern mothers; prefer it, they would, to a spray of johnny-jump-ups or trumpet vines.

"Then one—then one of the twelve Mother's Days would be—let's see—PMRD, Pay Mother's Rent Day. That wouldn't be bad. Pay Mother's Rent Day."

Father had a day, but Rogers declared that he could not remember when it was—"It's been so confused with April the First."

"This has been a great year for mothers. The Dionne quintuplets—that's been a great boost for motherhood. It's put motherhood on a mass-production basis. The mother of one lone chick has been made practically discouraged."

GREETS ENGLAND IN HONOR OF JUBILEE

Following his Mother's Day speech, Will Rogers was called upon to speak in the program sent across the ocean from this country in honor of the King's Jubilee in England. Again the radio audiences all over the world were privileged to hear another of Rogers' masterpieces of wit and wisdom.

"Hello, England!" Rogers said. "You have had a great week, haven't you? We read lots about it in our papers. You are ending your celebration today and I guess you are pretty well worn out.

"To make your fatigue complete, they have asked me to speak to you and without an interpreter.

"I imagine it is just about tea time over there. Well it's early in the A. M. over here. I am just drinking my coffee; you wouldn't know what that was. I mean I haven't had my breakfast yet. There are not many countries I would get up this early to talk to.

"I'd like to say right away, please don't mistake me for one of those self-styled good-will ambassadors. That's what's the matter with the relations between all nations today, is this bunk about good will. So get me right, England, I bring you no good will. You have, I know, been good-willed to death. I know we have over here.

"I am one speaker that brings you no message from America. America is so busy jumping from one scheme to another that we haven't any time to send a message to anybody. Anyone goin' or speakin' from one country to another says, 'I bring a message,' I don't think was ever authorized to do so by anybody else, and I am sure these millions of lecturers and authors that come from your country bringing us good will were not doing so by popular vote of the British Isles. And you might have voted for them to come over but not for that reason.

"I am just a humble admirer of a few of your— well, in fact, of many of your customs, and a great many of your people. I hope no one has ever judged my country by seeing me abroad, and perhaps you have sent as many nonrepresentative ones to us. Real people in both countries or in any country are the ones that stay at home.

"We both have manners and customs that drive each other pretty near crazy, and an American with a mouthful of chewing gum can get on your nerves almost as much as an Englishman with only one eyeful of monocle can get on ours, but, after all, neither commodity contributed to the success that these nations have made.

"You want no war with us, nor for that matter with anybody else. If you get new planes, our papers are full of it. If we get a new propeller for the old plane, we have your papers headline the fact saying it's war preparation.

"Anything of a war nature is all the foreign news that is printed in any country. In fact, every country has to read the papers every morning to see who you are sore at that day. Yet every nation must be doing many fine and beneficial and humanitarian things, but if it's not war, it's not in the other country's papers.

"We will never have trouble with each other, England, you or us. We both have humor. If we just started to fight, we'd have to stop in the middle and start laughing at each other. I don't know— you are naturally funny to us and we are like a Mickey Mouse cartoon to you.

"This jubilee is a great tribute to your King and your Queen, but it was their humanness that made the jubilee possible.　It wasn't the fact that they had ruled for twenty-five years.　You wasn't honoring years.　You were honoring people.　There has been a real man and woman and a King and Queen second.　Remove all the titles and you could remove all splendor and that couple, that great couple, with their families of children would be as representative a British family, as I imagine it would be possible for you to find in your whole empire.

"By the way, I don't believe he was over here even in his sailor days.　Maybe it was because nobody ever invited him there.　I know how it is with people like that.　I doubt if Roosevelt has ever been invited over there.　Big people think, 'Well they can't come,' so nobody goes to the trouble of thinking of inviting them.　We are kind of crude anyhow and maybe we have overlooked that.　I will take it on myself.

"We'd like to have the King and Queen come over here—always admire them.　They ought to see this country and everybody has left it to everybody else to do the inviting, so I'm going to do it.　Tell the Prince of Wales to get after them and do it.　He's a good guy.　Come over and see the country.

"Last summer I was there and got stepped on in Hyde Park when Mr. Mosley had his Black Shirts there.　It showed me England, like America, can never have communism, fascism, or nudism or any other ism.　Here was the Black Shirts and about a hundred yards away was the Communists, and in between was half of London laughing at both of them; and when I thought that was going to be a war, it ended quietly.

"They sang 'God Save the King' and all went home satisfied. They all had their say, and, after all, nobody wants his cause near as bad as he just wants to talk about his cause.

"England, you solved that problem. You certainly let 'em talk. I wish we would do a little more of that over here. We would let 'em get it off their minds.

"I saw you people when you were really under fire in the general strike of '26. It was the spirit of the way the people acted; no activity going on, yet everybody just as quiet and calm—the whole thing.

"And I was there during the Hatry trial which took place at the same time as the Disarmament Conference, when there was over one hundred newspapermen who left the conference—wasn't much doing there—and they went to the trial and wrote millions of words lauding English justice and the courts and the points of view of handling the giant swindler like that fellow Hatry was.

"Lots of my friends thought on account of my having so little tact I would be liable to mention something I shouldn't.

"Before I close, give my love to Lady Astor and Lloyd George. I know him. Give him my best regards and oh, Bernard Shaw, but don't tell him I left him to the last. He is kind of sensitive to little things like that. He devils the life out of you English folks but I know at heart he is kind of fond of you and he can't go back to Ireland.

"So, long life and happiness to your King and your Queen, and even if they don't come over, let us know if there is any chance of us joining you all on about the same terms as Canada is on."

FROM A FINAL BROADCAST

For one of his final broadcasts over a nation-wide network, Will Rogers visited Sacramento, California's capital, at a time when the Legislature was about to be adjourned for lack of funds.

"They just get paid for so many days, and then the money runs out," laughed Will. "There ain't nothing will dampen a man's public spirit more than to cut off his salary, you know.

"A lot of States have tried burnin' down the Capitol to get 'em out, but this way that California's got is the best way."

Commenting on the possibility that Roosevelt might intervene, he continued, "He kind of hates to see any place close down, so I wouldn't be surprised if he don't keep this thing going right on through, you know—like he does the CCC camps. He does that to keep the boys off the streets, and he's liable to give 'em money out here just to keep these State Senators off the same places."

A recent change in California's marriage laws provided him with an opportunity to create a good laugh.

"You know, when you got married in this State—you used to give three days' notice.

"That was longer than most of the marriages in California was lasting.

"So they did away with that. So now you don't have to file anything at all. In fact, you don't have to give your right name, according to this new law. You just pay a small amusement tax, that's all."

The California Legislature had voted to allow the Indians liquor, and Rogers, always proud of his Indian blood, was much amused.

"They passed one here to give the Indians their liquor. I don't mean you actually give 'em liquor but they're allowed to git it if they can. They're allowed to buy it.

"One old California cow-puncher from some county put that over. He told them we ought to give the Indians something back—the land or the liquor—so they compromised on the liquor. We kept the land and gave 'em the liquor. Lo, the poor Indian! The Indian, he's a ward to the Government, but we all are now. Everybody's an Indian."

That led to the latest news about Government relief grants to the States and Rogers congratulated Texas on drawing the "Grand Prize."

"Twenty-nine millions dollars last week—Texas did; New York got next prize of $24,000,000. Pennsylvania got third with $23,000,000. And they was all Republicans. Now I think that speaks awfully well of the Democrats. They're not going to let even a Republican starve."

Rogers suggested a reason why California did not get so much.

"We only got about $14,000,000 or something like that. Now I don't want to criticize—but I think

Mr. Hoover started to criticize a little too early, you know. I think that he knocked us out of ten or fifteen million there. You can't knock the man that's paying you."

On this broadcast, Rogers had as his guest the famous humorist, Irvin S. Cobb. He interviewed Cobb on several things.

ROGERS: What do you do to keep your weight down?

COBB: I don't keep my weight down. It's my weight that is keeping me down.

ROGERS: Do you find yourself going Hollywood in any way, you know?

COBB: Well, I find that I'm talking to myself—and worse than that, I'm answering back.

ROGERS: Kind of saying your own yesses?

COBB: Yes. I am living in Yes Man's Land which is worse than No Man's Land during the war.

ROGERS: Do you find that this censorship that Will Hays has got in on us now is—does it kind of interfere with you—sort of—

COBB: Well, I notice they've begun talking about putting a tax on raw film.

ROGERS: Did you ever see Mae West?

COBB: Yes, once years ago, but I won't talk about that. Apparently everybody that used to know Mae West claims they married her.

CHAPTER VII

ROGERS AS A WRITER

WHEN I first started out to write and mis-spelled a few words, people said I was just plain ignerant. But when I got all the words wrong, they declared I was a humorist, and said I was quaint."

That was Will Rogers' own description of his writing career but it was far more complex than that. His writings represented the shrewd obser-vations that rushed through his mind, and so adept was Rogers at coating a sound idea with a little humor that they were read daily by hundreds of thousands of persons. On all his journeyings around the world, Will carried his portable type-writer and each day he sat down and picked out, with two fingers, "a piece for the papers." In addition, he wrote feature articles and several books. His total output was enormous and, naturally, some of it did not quite measure up to the high standard that he actually set for himself. Viewed in the light of the fact that his writings, like his sayings, were meant for immediate consumption and were not intended to go ringing down through the cor-ridors of time, the finished product bore the hall-mark of rare genius. It was the sincerest tribute that other "sagebrush" and "homespun" philoso-phers aped his style, even to the phonetic spelling, but their ruminations lacked the ring of genuineness, and offered no more serious competition than did the imitators of his vaudeville days. There could be only one Will Rogers.

POPULAR COMMENTATOR ON NEWS

It was shortly after Will became a sensation on Broadway as a commentator on the news of the day, that V. V. McNitt, president of the McNaught Newspaper Syndicate, went to the Amsterdam Theater and listened to his act. Realizing that Rogers' remarks would make a first-class newspaper feature, McNitt sought out the Oklahoman and suggested the idea. Rogers insisted he couldn't write but was willing "to try." The try-out was a success from the very beginning and at the end of his career his newspaper earnings were said to be of such proportions that they made him one of the highest priced syndicate writers in the history of journalism.

In the twenty years that he wrote for the McNaught Syndicate he missed only two days. Once he was in Mexico far away from a telegraph station, and the other time he was in the hospital undergoing an operation. It was said that Will's articles had the greatest reader circulation of any published in the world. And Rogers loved to write. Frequently he expressed the idea that he would like to give up the motion-pictures business and go jaunting around the world in an airplane as an "aërial reporter," commenting upon whatever struck his fancy wherever he chanced to be.

ROGERS' "DAILY CHORE"

He never wrote his articles in advance and regardless of whether he was on a movie location or in a distinguished gathering he would excuse himself and say: "I've got to do my daily chore." Then he would sit down and write the article that was to be published the next day. As nimble as his fingers were at spinning ropes, Will never mastered the handling of carbon papers, and consequently never made any duplicates of what he wrote. If the article was mislaid, he had to turn around and write a new one.

At first he wrote only a weekly news feature that was published in the Sunday newspapers, but in 1926, a chance cable query sent by Rogers from London to the New York *Times* started him on the writing of a daily "box," a short feature set apart from the rest of the news by black lines. Rogers asked the *Times* if they would pay the cable tolls on a brief message. He was told immediately that the tolls would be paid, and a short time later the following message came clicking across the Atlantic Ocean:

"Nancy Astor, which is the nom de plume of Lady Astor, is arriving on your side about now. She is the best friend America has here. Please ask my friend Jimmy Walker to have New York take good care of her. She is the only one over here that don't throw rocks at American tourists.

"Yours respectfully,

"WILL ROGERS."

Ordinarily the message would have been placed on the editorial page in the "Letters to the Editor" column but Joseph Tebeau, night managing editor, placed it in a "box" on the front page of the second news section. Each day a message came from Rogers and this continued for four months, until October, 1926, when he returned. Will received no remuneration for this daily feature up to that time, but by then it was one of the most valuable syndicate features ever conceived.

SELF-MADE DIPLOMAT

The meeting with Lady Astor that prompted the sending of the cablegram to the New York *Times* was brought about through George H. Lorimer, editor of *The Saturday Evening Post*. Rogers had written a series of articles for tne *Post*, entitled "Letters of a Self-made Diplomat to His President," that had won wide acclaim and when he was going to England, Lorimer gave him a letter of introduction to Lady Astor.

When Rogers presented the letter at her home in London, according to the story, Lady Astor told her maid she did not know him and that she would dismiss him in ten minutes, as she had to attend a very important political meeting. After talking with the "self-made diplomat," she invited him to attend the meeting. Rogers went and there she called upon him to speak to the gathering. He met with such approval that during his stay in London, Lady Astor insisted upon him accompanying her on all of her political tours.

The articles written as a result of that trip abroad were later compiled in one of his most successful books. It was in two volumes and bore the same title as the magazine features. In the preface, he wrote:

"Writing today is based on endurance not thought, and I am going to give my public the advantage of a wonderful physical constitution while it's at its peak. I know when you read this volume you will say: 'I want Volume Number Two, it must be better.'"

Commenting on the trip, Rogers said:

"My trip came at a time when foreign relations were at their most perilous peak; that is, when we were trying to collect money. Any man can fight a war, but it takes a smart man to jar any loose change out of any part of Europe, especially when they have already eat up the money that was loaned them. But my mission will always stand out, because it is much easier for America to whip a nation than it is to collect a dollar from them. I have to go abroad when we are as welcome as rent collectors. There is only one way we could be in worse with Europeans, and that is to have helped them out of two wars instead of one."

PRINCE OF WALES A "REGULAR FELLER"

While in London that year, Rogers renewed his acquaintanceship with the Prince of Wales, for whom he had the greatest of admiration as one of the most "regular fellers" he ever met.

"One thing that I want you to know that will establish his character better than anything else,"

Rogers wrote, "and show you that he has a real sense of humor is when I first come in I said: 'Hello, old timer. How are you falling these days?' and he replied as quick as a flash: 'All over the place. I got my shoulder broke since I saw you last.'"

The Prince at that time had gone in for steeple-chase riding and hunting. He was thrown several times when the horses fell on perilous jumps and his accidents were a matter of grave concern in Great Britain. In the United States, however, comedians and humorists seized upon his tumbles as a rich source of material for jokes and gags.

"I hear you are a journalist now," the Prince said. "This is no interview, remember; just renewing old acquaintanceship."

"Anything you say to me is just *ad lib*," Rogers replied, "and nobody will ever know it but President Coolidge and America."

For pure, unadulterated American wit, Rogers was in a class by himself, but there were fun makers who were envious of his great talent and once the rumor was circulated along Broadway that he did not "write his own stuff." The rumor mongers argued that no one man could turn out such a prodigious amount of copy and have most of it so good. The reports came to Rogers and as far as known, he made only one passing comment on them. That was the night the stagehands of the Amsterdam Theater gave him a surprise party on his birthday.

As Will stood at the head of the festive board, he was visibly impressed by the thoughtfulness of his hosts and he remarked:

"All I can say, boys, is that I wish the feller that writes my stuff was here to talk for me."

LITERARY ACHIEVEMENTS

Will's first book, *Rogerisms,* was published in 1919 and the same year also appeared *The Cowboy Philosopher on the Peace Conference* and *The Cowboy Philosopher on Prohibition.* The following year *Rogerisms—What We Laugh At* was published and then for several years he confined himself solely to his newspaper work.

Once Will was writing the material for a motion picture weekly feature called "The Illiterate Digest." The widely read news weekly, *The Literary Digest,* at that time was showing on the screen a short film called *Topics of the Day,* after the department in its columns. These "topics" consisted of pithy sayings and epigrams culled from the editorial columns of the newspapers all over the world. Some legal light connected with the *Digest* thought Rogers' feature was an encroachment upon their film and wrote the humorist a letter concerning it.

Rogers' reply said: "Your letter in regard to my competition with *The Literary Digest* received and I never felt as swelled up in my life." He then went on to explain that he had stopped the short feature because "the gentlemen who put it out were behind in their payments, and my humor kinder waned, in fact after a few weeks of no payments I couldn't think of a single joke."

Four years later, in 1924, his book called *Illiterate Digest* was published and it contained many of the

humorous sayings he had written for the movie
feature.

Two years later he wrote his famous "letters"
and this was followed by *There's Not a Bathing
Suit in Russia,* which was a shrewd and humorous
account of his first visit to Soviet Russia.   Despite
his lampooning, his observations made many friends
among the powerful Russian leaders.

It was during his tour of Europe by steamship
and airplane that the legend arose of his visit to
Buckingham Palace.   It is probably apocryphal, but
it could have happened to him.

"I'm Will Rogers and I've come to see the King,"
Will is supposed to have said to the guards.

"Tell the King that when the Prince of Wales was
over in our country not long ago, he told me to look
up his old man and here I am."

According to the story, Rogers was admitted and
was invited by King George and Queen Mary to
stay to lunch.

40,000,000 READERS

It was to be expected that in writing for 350 daily
and 200 Sunday newspapers from coast to coast
some of his estimated 40,000,000 readers would find
fault with some of his opinions.   That happened in
November, 1932, when he expressed his ideas concerning the war debt situation.   The New York
Times received a number of protests, and in an
editorial set forth the general idea that Rogers'
writings were his own opinion and not to be construed
as the editorial policy of the *Times*.

Rogers retorted promptly and the *Times* printed it in the space that was given to his comments. It read:

"Beverly Hills, Calif., Dec. 7.—I would like to state to the readers of the New York *Times* that I am in no way responsible for the editorial or political policy of this paper.

"I allow them free reign as to their opinion, so long as it is within the bounds of good subscription gathering.

"But I want it distinctly understood that their policy may be in direct contrast to mine.

"Their editorials may be put in purely for humor, or just to fill space.

"Every paper must have its various entertaining features, and their editorials are not always to be taken seriously, and never to be construed as my policy.

"Yours,

"WILL ROGERS."

There was no sham or bluff about Rogers in either his writings or his speech. Success with his typewriter never turned a single hair on his head any more than his achievements on the stage, screen, or lecture platform. Someone suggested to him that he took too many liberties with the laws of syntax.

"What's syntax?" asked Rogers. "Sounds like bad news."

"I mean you use bad grammar." replied his companion.

"Shucks," declared Rogers. "I didn't know they was buyin' grammar now. I'm just so dumb I had a notion it was thoughts and ideas. I write just like I talk. If there's bad grammar, it ain't intentional."

RECIPE FOR HUMOR

Rogers' recipe for humor also was characteristic of the man. It was simple and undoubtedly the way he fashioned countless witticisms that came from his tongue and typewriter. He forgot to add, however, that ingredients should be well mixed with his own particular type of brains. The "recipe" follows:

"A gag to be any good has to be fashioned about some truth. The rest you get by your slant on it and perhaps by a wee bit of exaggeration, so's people won't miss the point."

The Rogers' "slant" on things was the factor that those who tried to copy his style could never find. His weekly articles which appeared in the Sunday newspapers throughout the country invariably started, "Well, all I know is just what I read in the papers." He would then proceed to show that in reading the newspapers he gleaned far more information than the average reader ever suspected they contained.

Frequently, however, Rogers showed the strong sentimental side of himself in his writings, and when he did, he forgot to jibe at the fads and foibles of the day. For example, he wrote the following for his weekly feature for the McNaught Syndicate:

"I had a funny kind of a trip two or three weeks ago. My younger kid Jimmy and my little nephew, Jimmy Blake, were over in the panhandle of Texas on the Mashed O Ranch learning to be cowboys. They were having a big calf branding. The ranch belongs to the Halsell Family, old family friends of my folks and myself. It's where I went a couple of years ago and was roping calves, and an old jug-headed gray horse I was riding got tangled in the rope, and the calf and I was just an innocent bystander.

"All I got out of it was being bucked off on my head. On account of using good judgment in knowing how to fall, why I wasn't hurt at all. The old horse stampeded around the corral with the calf anchored to him and tore up the branding fire. All this time I was just scratching old cut-off ear marks and other amputated parts out of my hair. An old, dry cowpuncher (and I never saw many that wasn't) said, 'Well you will sho have something to write about now.' He figured here is a day when he will lay off the Republicans and tell something amusing.

"Well this time I flew out there one night. Flew all night and got to Amarillo at four o'clock in the morning. It's about 100 miles to the ranch, down at a town named Muleshoe (I suppose it's an old Spanish name and came from the thing a mule wears on his foot). Well, I got in a taxi and lit out. I figured there wasn't much time to sleep, so I told the old boy, 'Let's get some breakfast and then hit on out of town.' I dident know the road, but I did know the direction. . . .

"We went by the restaurant to get ham and eggs, for out West everything you do you must get ham and eggs first. Then when you get it done, you get ham and eggs again. An old girl and her beau (perhaps) eating in there too about 4.30 that morning, she recognized me. She had on an evening dress, that's mighty late for an evening dress in Amarillo. She wanted me to join her in what she said was a cup of coffee 'that had something in it.' I told her I was doing mighty well on this coffee I had ordered that had nothing but grounds in it. But she swore she was drinking 'Coffee Royal.' That sounded awful 'Continental' to be browsing around in Amarillo. Why even 'Old Tack' never heard of that.

"Well, anyhow, she got plum sore at me because I wouldent join her. And when I said 'Good Morning' as my driver and me went out, she turned her bare back on me and muttered, 'Them actors are all alike, they are all swell headed, that's what I get for speaking to a ham. He dident know a lady when he seen one.'

"Well as it got to getting daylight and we passed all those little frame farmhouses on every prairie quarter section, (where it never in the world should have been plowed up) I never saw as many fowls of various breeds try to cross the road ahead of us. Chickens, turkeys, guinea hens. This old driver boy looked like he took fiendish delight in trying to maim some of 'em, but much to my delight he couldent reach any of em.

"We was driving over a country where thirty-six years before as a boy eighteen years old, I had helped drive a bunch of cattle from that very place to western Kansas, and there wasent a house or a chicken in the whole county. That plains was the prettiest country I ever saw in my life, as flat as a beauty contest winner's stomach, and prairie lakes scattered all over it. And mirages! You could see anything in the world—just ahead of you—I eat out of a chuck wagon, and slept on the ground all that spring and summer of '98. (Lot of folks went to the Klondike, but I couldent get any farther away from my home in the Indian Territory than Texas.) The limit of my 'Pay Dirt' was I think thirty dollars a month.

"Well here I was thirty-six years later driving out to a ranch, to eat at another 'Chuck Wagon,' and do a little roping. A good deal had happened to everybody in thirty-six years. No more happens to one person than to another. Some look bigger, but they are no bigger than the things that look little that happens to the other fellow."

"ALL I KNOW I READ IN THE PAPERS"

Another typical column of comment, written for the McNaught Syndicate, shows how he skipped blithely from one subject to another as his fancy dictated. It read:

"Well all I know is just what I read in the papers. Congress just keeps us all on the jump all the time, waiting to see what they are going to do with us. One minute they are not going to have a sales tax.

but they put a tax on about a third of the things that are sold. Then they were asked to explain why it was that they taxed a boot, but dident tax a shoe, or why put a tax on caps but none on hats. That is just about as nonsensikle as the things they did do."

* * *

"Well it just looks like Congress took a list of everything made and shut their eyes and took a pencil and marked off some names, and said, 'We will tax everything the pencil marks across.' "

* * *

"They been investigating Wall Street, but there has been so much devilment going on there that one Committee can't dig it all out. They wanted to publish the names of the Firms that were implicated in the 'Bear Raids,' and the list was twenty-four thousand."

* * *

"England come out with their Budget and it dident make any allowance for paying their debts to us. Well, we come out with our Budget without paying our debt to ourselves. We can't seem to find any dough to do anything with, but England hadent any more than broke out till Senator Borah was right on their trail. He reminded 'em that there had been an oversight on somebody's part.

"You see thats the trouble; you just can't do a nation a favor, or they will want it continued, although I will say this England will pay, and did, quicker than any the rest of 'em."

* * *

"France just has guys laying awake at night to think up reasons for not paying. They give guys percentage on every new idea he gets for new reasons. France's main reason now is that if she paid us, she would have to use her gold, and if she had to use her gold, she wouldent have as much gold. But England is a different breed of cats altogether. The old Englishman is a mighty high-type business man.

"Well, we will hear a lot about it anyhow, for it will be starting to come due in a few months, and the campaign this fall will be so full of debt arguments that you will think the future of the country hinged on the outcome."

* * *

"Hollywood is all excited, they hear Greta Garbo is going home, she might be at home for all we know, nobody has ever seen her out here. In fact she may make her pictures over there and just be sending 'em over.

"She is supposed to go home now and take up this match king job. He was the biggest man over there. And she is the biggest woman. So they figure she could put it on its feet. Say, by the way, that old boy sure put one over on 'em, dident he? Talk about us having some slick 'Hombres,' why Europe can make a sucker out of us for 'Fenagling' guys."

* * *

"This depression has brought out a lot of crooked stuff where if things had gone on and they had been able to keep covering up they would never have been known.

"Talk about running a car into a billion dollars, why just think of running a little tiny stick of wood, with some phospherous on the end of it into an establishment that controlled the finances of a dozen nations.

"We all just kinder sitting around here waiting for the new cars to be delivered, that about the only event in our lives. We trade in the old ones and go in debt for the differences.

"We are all talking Olympic games out here. We dont know what they do or how they do it, but we want to see it. Fifty-five nations are coming. It will either be a success or a war, so in either case you dont want to miss it.

"There is hundreds of women competing, only in this case they have to compete against each other, and not just against the men. Its going to be well worth seeing. Come on out, you are not doing anything, anyhow. If you run a store or are in business, why put your customer in the car and bring him too then you wont lose him.

"Remember the date? Well I forgot when it was myself, but its sometime during the hot weather."

ROGERS GENUINELY SYMPATHETIC

The serious side of Will Rogers was shown to the public whenever disaster overtook some section of the country. He would appeal to the public to be generous to the unfortunates and the untold good he accomplished in that manner never can be measured. When Charles A. Lindbergh, Jr., was kidnaped from his crib and cruelly murdered by a beast of a man, Rogers sounded the feeling of the country when he wrote:

"What a shock to everybody; but how much more of a one it is when you have seen the baby and seen the affection of the mother and father and the whole Morrow family for the cute little fellow.

"Two weeks ago Sunday Mrs. Rogers and I spent the day with them. The whole family interest centered around him. He had his father's blond curly hair. It's almost golden and in little curls. His face is more of his mother's. He has her eyes exactly.

"His mother sat on the floor in the sun parlor among all of us and played blocks with him for an hour. . . . He crawled up in the back of the Morrow automobile that was going to take us home, and he howled like an Indian when they dragged him out.

"I wish we had taken him home with us and kept him."

* * *

It was in his daily comments, however, that Will reached the heights as a satirist on the affairs of the moment. The following was written just prior to the Presidential election in 1932, when Franklin D. Roosevelt defeated President Hoover:

"Los Angeles, Calif., Nov. 2.—Come pretty near having two holidays of equal importance in the same week, Halloween and election, and of the two election provides us the most fun. On Halloween they put pumpkins on their heads, and on election they don't have to.

"Candidates have been telling you that if elected they would 'pull you from this big hole of financial misery.' Now is a good chance to get even with 'em, by electing 'em, just to prove what a liar they are.

"Personally I think this is the right year for a good man to be defeated in.

"Yours,

"WILL ROGERS."

SHAFTS OF WIT

The wide range of subjects at which he aimed his sugar-coated shafts of wit is exemplified in the following excerpts taken from his newspaper writings:

"There is far more pride involved at this naval conference than ships. The minute you rate a nation, they naturally think you're establishing their importance in comparison to everybody else. . . . So remember it's not tonnage they are prorating, it's prestige. If they only had to divide up ships, they would be home next week."

* * *

"Every invention during our lifetime has been just to save time. . . . Two hundred years from now history will record: 'America, a nation that flourished from 1900–1942, conceived many odd inventions for getting somewhere, but could think of nothing to do when they got there.'"

* * *

"If I wanted to start an insane asylum that would be 100 per cent cuckoo, I would just admit applicants that thought they knew something about Russia."

* * *

"Another disarmament conference disbanded in Geneva without doing anything but getting more suspicious of each other. If any two nations don't hate each other, why just let them confer on something. And they will before it's over. Stop conferring and you will stop fighting."

* * *

"1930 was a year of "under and over-estimation." Nothing was guessed right all year. Optimism was over-rated and pessimism was under-rated."

* * *

"We don't seem to be able to even check crime, so why not legalize it and put a heavy tax on it? Make the tax for robbery so high that a bandit couldn't afford to rob anyone unless he knew they had a lot of dough. We have taxed other industries out of business; it might work here."

* * *

"Back home from South America. Must be American territory—I don't see any marines."

* * *

"Calvin Coolidge was the only man in America that saw this whole thing coming, and got from under. He just says to himself: 'Folks have bought everything in the world, for a dollar down, under me, now let them pay for them under Herbert.'"

* * *

"Here is about how Manchuria looks to me: China owns the lot. Japan owns the house that's on it. Now who should have the policemen? China is trying to save its country. Japan is trying to save its investments. The League of Nations is trying to save its face."

* * *

"I would like to stay in Europe long enough to find some country that don't blame America for everything in the world that's happened to 'em in the last fifteen years—debts, depression, disarmament, disease, fog, famine, or frostbite."

* * *

"I see where some line is going to make aviation pay by taking it out of the pilot's salary. When they start hiring cheap pilots, I will stop flying."

* * *

"Out on the Rogers Ranch at Oologah, where I spent yesterday, Herb McSpadden, my nephew, had to take a milk stool and whack an old cow over the rear end. She was hoarding her milk."

* * *

"Everybody you talk to would rather hear about Capone than anybody you ever met. What's the matter with an age when our biggest gangster is our greatest national interest? Part is the government's fault for not convicting him on some real crime."

* * *

"Headline says, 'Society Women of New York Smoking Pipe.' The only way to break 'em from it is not to watch 'em do it."

* * *

"Here I go and make a week's mistake in my time, and arrive back in the midst of the most colossal rodeo of applesauce in the history of our national pastime. I honestly believe there is people so excited over this election that they think the President has something to do with running the country."

* * *

"Mr. Hoover, the consolation you have from the whole American people is no doubt greater than that ever shared by a losing President. There was nothing personal in the vote against you. You just happened to be associated with a political party that the people had lost their taste for. We all know that you was handed a balloon that was blowed up to its utmost. You held it as carefully as anyone could, but the thing busted right in your hands. Well, there ain't just much we can do in a case like that."

* * *

"America hasn't been as happy in three years as they are today. No money, no banks, no work, no nothing, but they know they got a man in there who is wise to Congress and wise to our so-called big men. The whole country is with him. Even if what he does is wrong they are with him. Just so he does something. If he burned down the Capitol, we would cheer and say, 'Well, we at least got a fire started anyhow.'"

* * *

"Washington has got 'Coditis' . . . This old Oklahoma Johnson is in there and he is papa in

Washington now. You bring your code to him.
He uncodes it, recodes you another one, you sign it,
get you a bluebird and go back in business again.''

* * *

"Flew in (Washington) this afternoon to see what
the boys who live by the ballot box are doing.
They're busy as usual passing appropriation bills
like hot biscuits at a country farm house. . . .
Snowed here, but you can't see the ground for the
lobbyists.''

* * *

"From all I can read in the papers, dated from
some foreign capital, the ambition of their lives
seems to be to force us and Japan into a war. Now,
if any nation on earth can give any excuse why we
should fight Japan anymore than they should, they
ought to get a prize for thinking of it.''

* * *

"The greatest aid that I know of that any man
could give the world today would be a correct
definition of 'liberty.' Everybody is running around
in a circle announcing that somebody has pinched
their 'liberty.' . . . . So the question arises 'how
much liberty can I get and get away with it?'
Well you can get no more than you give. That's
my definition but you got perfect 'liberty' to work
out your own, so get in.''

* * *

"I visited (the Louisiana) Capitol today. . . .
They have buttons on the desks and they vote by
electricity. It's a marvelous way to vote, but

Huey runs the switchboard, so it don't matter much which button the boys press, all the answers come out yes."

* * *

"A holding company is a thing where you hand an accomplice the goods while the policeman searches you."

* * *

"The trouble with the Versailles peace treaty is that the men that made it are dead, and the ones living say, 'We didn't sign that mortgage.' "

* * *

"This Alaska is a great country. If they can just keep from being taken over by the United States they got a great future. . . . There may be some doubt about the Louisiana Purchase being a mistake, but when Seward in '68 bought Alaska for $7,000,000 he even made up for what we had over-paid the Indians for Manhattan Island."

* * *

"Visited our new immigrants. . . . As I see it, there is not but one problem now that they are here, and that's to get 'em housed within six or eight weeks. Things have been in a terrible mess. They are getting 'em straightened out, but even now not fast enough. . . . There is plenty food and always has been and will be. They can always get that in, but it's houses they need right now and Colonel Hunt, in charge, realizes it. You know, after all, there is a lot of difference in pioneering for gold and pioneering for spinach."

CHAPTER VIII

AMBASSADOR OF GOOD WILL

COWBOYS and statesmen, peasants and princes, movie extras and stars, paupers and millionaires, were all one to Will Rogers. Riches in great abundance poured into his coffers. He was fêted by the wealthy and by royalty. But he never lost the common touch. He could dine in a palace, but he would just as soon sit down on the ground and munch a sandwich with a laborer on the movie lot. The Prince of Wales laughed at his witticisms but they were relished equally by the sidling panhandler, who "bummed" him for a dime to buy a cup of coffee. John D. Rockefeller was his friend, but so was the lowest "extra" in one of his movies. Andrew Mellon chuckled at Will's sage remarks but so did the counter man at the all-night "one-armed" lunchroom where Rogers frequently stopped for a bite to eat.

He could talk anyone's language, for he was a friend to the world, but he always carefully explained that while he joked about the wealthy, the statesmen, the socially elect, and royalty he "didn't look down upon 'em."

"They'd be just as good as anybody else if they had an equal chance," he declared.

Will Rogers scaled the heights in diplomacy and "society" when the Prince of Wales "commanded"

Will Rogers and Mrs. Rogers repay a visit in Tokyo, Japan, to Takamaru Konoe, son of Prince Fumimaro Konoe, whom Will Rogers first met in America.

In an elaborate ceremony, in which he received a floral key of the city, Will Rogers was inducted into office as honorary mayor of Beverly Hills.

him in 1924 to attend a dinner at the Long Island
Country Club during the Prince's visit to this
country. The Prince had heard Rogers in London
and wanted to meet him. All the others at the
dinner appeared in the strictest of formal attire but
Will arrived at the club wearing his worn, blue serge
suit and sat down beside the Prince. And, it must
be recorded, that despite his lack of correct evening
wear he "stole the show" from the Prince. As the
repast progressed, Rogers and the Prince kept up a
running fire of conversation. The Prince laughed
heartily at Will's jests and when the "ambassador
without portfolio" arose to talk, he made the Prince
his one and only target. The heir to England's
throne enjoyed it to the uttermost and occasionally
leaned over to twitch Rogers' coattail and whisper,
"Tell them that one you told me about——"

"Best feeder I ever had," Rogers declared afterward. "He plugged my act and furnished material
at the same time."

After the Prince returned to England, Rogers, in
his weekly news feature for the McNaught Syndicate,
wrote:

"Well, the Prince left us. We had no more got
rid of him until La Follette came. They just will
not let New York settle down to normal. You often
hear the expression that a person has left the country
flat, but this case of the Prince's departure was the
only one in history where he left the country asleep.
Long Island went to bed the night he left and has
not woke up yet; in fact, they didn't even leave a
call. You won't be able to promote another dance

on Long Island for years. A lot of men got their wives back much shopworn from dancing. The Prince left a trail of broken hearts and turned-down hats that won't be forgotten for weeks."

"AMBASSADOR" ROGERS

Kings, dictators, presidents, diplomats, prime ministers, and leaders everywhere were friends of Rogers. They all enjoyed his sharp, shrewd observations on the events of the day in their countries.

King George, Von Hindenburg, Mussolini, Stalin, the late King Albert, Stanley Baldwin, Lloyd George, Clemenceau, President Calles—the list could go on and on until all the top flight of the leaders of the world were included—knew the unofficial "ambassador" from the United States. It would be politic, of course, for those in the know to deny it, but it was more than once rumored that Rogers' journeys around the world were not mere pleasure jaunts but visits that had a very serious purpose behind them. Whether there was such a motive, and it does not seem unlikely, Rogers found in these trips material for witticisms that added to his stature as a commentator on international affairs. None of the recognized students of world affairs ever achieved the recognition from the general public that he did, nor were they able to convey the news as Rogers did in homeopathic capsules of misspelled words.

Will came back from a world tour in 1926 with doleful comments of the Administration troubles in Nicaragua, Mexico, and China, all of which he ascribed to a meddling desire to be "helpful."

"Every time we start out on a humanitarian mission, we come back with both legs in a sling.

"Get the humor of our going to Nicaragua to settle an election.   Personally, I think Nicaragua did pretty good with the little money they've got. Nicaragua is a poor country; one little precinct in Philadelphia did better at the last election.   We ought to give them money down there so that they can put on real elections, something like ours.

"As for Tacna-Arica, most of us don't know whether Tacna-Arica is the name of a country or a mouth wash.

"Now we are messing around with China.   You can't even get a gunboat now if you want to take a little excursion; all our gunboats are somewhere up the Yangtze River.   Remember, China never bothered any nation in the world.   I ain't up on history, but China had civilization three thousand years before there was anything here—and I never heard of China invading anyone's country.   These Chinese get mighty few pleasures out of life so they thought they'd have a civil war.   And they can't even have that without us and England hornin' in on it.   Just like two old busybodies—that's what England and America are.

"When we had our Civil War, some Chinese laundryman might have got a bullet in his neck; still China didn't step in, collect our customs for us, and send gunboats up the Mississippi River.   Why don't we let 'em have their war?

"Now we've got a lot of missionaries in China. The missionaries have done at least one thing—

they've got the Chinese educated up to civil war. Right now they're all flocking to Shanghai to be safe. I should think they'd all start now converting each other.

"Not only in Nicaragua, Mexico, and China, but in Europe, the American goes where he isn't welcome. Our tourists spent seven hundred millions to be insulted in Europe last year. We're the only nation that goes where we're not wanted. Even at the League of Nations where we don't belong, we peek in unofficially with the unofficial observers."

In describing his trip to Rome and his interview with Mussolini, he said: "I stood in the Roman Forum and I found out that they had a Senate in Rome long ago. That's why Rome declined. Boy! If they declined with a Senate, what will we do with a Senate and a House."

Rogers was known the world over because of his motion pictures, and his travels in the numerous countries he visited were something like triumphal tours. In 1932 he flew to South America, and in October of that year while on his way home, the plane was forced down by a storm on the outskirts of Santos, a city in the coffee-growing district of Brazil. When the natives rushed out, they recognized Rogers at once.

He was forced to stay in the town overnight and it was arranged that he appear at a local theater. Will couldn't speak Portuguese, and they couldn't understand English, but he produced a lariat and proceeded to give them a demonstration of roping tricks that spoke a language they all understood.

On the way back to the United States he stopped at Havana, Cuba, where he was the guest of honor at a dinner given by Captain Demarest, American Consul at Cuba. It seems of more than passing significance that all the embassies at the Cuban capital were represented.

THE OLD BLUE SERGE

Will appeared at the dinner in his old blue serge suit. The ambassadors and consuls present were there in full "regimentals," with their medals and ribbons, giving a very colorful atmosphere to the dinner. Rogers, when called upon, proceeded to "denounce boiled shirts" for evening dress in the tropics.

The Chinese minister listened to Rogers' jokes and when he had finished, it was observed that the Oriental hurriedly quit the banquet room. After the repast an impromptu concert was put on for Will's entertainment. It had just about started when the Chinese minister walked into the room attired in an informal tropical suit of silk. The fashionable gathering applauded and Will grinned.

"I shall be offended," Rogers told that gathering, "if anyone accuses me of making a good-will tour to Cuba. I believe the honest policy of trade of the West Indies business men requires no commercial diplomacy."

Rogers was the guest of honor on similar occasions in Shanghai, Moscow, and even in far-away Siam.

"A great place, Siam, but puzzling," Rogers remarked. "I didn't see the king, but his father-in-law and mother-in-law gave me a party.   His father-in-law is his uncle.   Don't try to figure that out."

In commenting upon Russian affairs, Rogers said, "Russia's a country that used to have four exports —dukes, grand dukes, princesses, and whiskers."

Of Stalin he commented: "Of course, him being a dictator, he's allowed certain extensive privileges. The government in Russia owns everything.   Well, that ain't so different than over here.   The banks own it over here.

"I am about the only person that ever talked about Russia that admits that I don't know anything about it," Rogers said.   "And on the other hand I know just as much about it as everybody that ever talked about it.   Nobody knows anything about Russia.   It's too complicated."

OBSERVATIONS ON CHINA

In one of his Sunday feature articles he masked some exceedingly astute observations on China in a glowing eulogy of Pearl Buck, noted novelist. Rogers wrote:

"Well all I know is just what I read in the papers, or what I run onto here and there.   I was just sitting here a while ago reading a long article about Pearl Buck, the author of those books about Chinese life.   Just a few days before leaving New York prior to the election, Mrs. Rogers and I had the pleasure of spending an hour or more with this very remarkable woman.   How it come about was that last year when I was over in China, I had read one of

her books on the boat, when I wasent arguing with
Floyd Gibbons. Well, I thought it was the greatest
thing I had ever read, so I talked to lots of people
over there about her.   A Dr. Donaldson, whom I
met on the train from Peking to Shanghai, had known
the family of this girl for years. He and they both
were early missionaries out there.

"I wanted to meet her while out there. She lived
up at Nanking; that's the capital of China, or was
that week. It used to be Peking, and if the southern
crowd keep getting stronger, I guess it will be
Canton.

"I wanted to go up to Nanking anyhow. I had
come through there on the train from Peking, but
dident get to see much. So I called up the school
where they live. Her husband [former] is a prcfessor
in a big university there. He has made a study of
agriculture and is a graduate of Cornell.

"By the way, that always struck me as being the
oddest place for an agriculture course. You just
kinder look for them out in the Middle West, where
they raise something. I got in communication with
them up at Nanking and was to go up and see her
on a certain day. I was going to fly. There was
a line of sea planes that went right up the Yangtse
River. I got to the place to take off that day, and
it was raining and cloudy all day, so I dident get
to go.

"I was leaving on the boat the next day for Singa-
pore, then for the flight across India, and all points
West. I talked to Mr. Buck, her husband, over the
phone, but not seeing her out there was a great

disappointment, for she is one person that wrote a book about a country, and even that country liked it. I never heard a derogatory (that's a pretty hot word for me, ain't it?) word about the book. The Chinese say it was true to life and character.

"Her publishers knew what a great admirer I was of hers, so when I landed from South America and Mrs. Rogers met me in New York, why they phoned us and said Mrs. Buck would be in New York at a certain time and would see us.

"We were tickled to death. We went over to her hotel. Her husband is taking a special course again at Cornell. He is quite an agricultural authority in China, and has held some very important Government missions in regard to trying to get them straightened out on what to raise. She, too, I think, was taking some course up there. So she stayed there most all the time. She just come down to New York occasionally; she dident like it so much. She is not so hot for this hero-worship business. She is very modest and wonderfully interesting to talk to. She almost speaks with an accent, she has spoken Chinese so long.

"After *Sons*, which was another powerful book, she is working on the third and last of the series. . . You know if you know your Chinese, there is quite a big communistic hold in certain parts of China. The influence is growing rapidly. They want her to show that it will be through communism that China will eventually be saved. I don't know what they are supposed to be saved from, for they have the best mode of life and living in the world now.

Will Rogers was never happier than he was when roping wild steers at his ranch near Santa Monica.

The usual procedure was reversed this time when Will Rogers gave the Oil
King a dime.

"But somebody is always saving China from something or other. She said in *The Good Earth* that while she dident write it in Chinese, that her thoughts were all in Chinese; that is, her characters were all talking to each other in Chinese. Then, as she translated the very words into English, before writing them down, some of the reviewers got the idea that it was Old Testament writing, or a throw-back to her missionary training. She denies that and says it came from these words being the very ones the Chinese utter, in a literal translation."

LETTERS OF A SELF-MADE DIPLOMAT

One classic that Will Rogers wrote on international affairs was printed in *The Saturday Evening Post* in 1926 and later in his book *Letters of a Self-made Diplomat to His President*. In it he said: "We don't stand like a horse thief abroad. Whoever told you that is flattering us. We don't stand as good as a horse thief.

"These guys over here are so busy celebrating our unpopularity that they don't stop to look around to see how they stand themselves. If you can find me one nation in Europe that has a sincere regard for any other nation, I will jump out of the top of Washington Monument and see if Jackie Coogan can catch me as I fall.

"France and England think as much of each other as two rival bands of Chicago bootleggers. . . . Spain and France have the same regard for each other as Fort Worth and Dallas. . . . Russia hates everybody so bad it would take her a week to pick

out the one she hates most. . . . Poland is rarin' to
fight. . . . Turkey has been laying off three months
now without any war and peace is just killin'
them. . . . Bulgaria is feeding an army and deriving
no benefits whatever. . . . Greece has open time
they are trying to fill in. . . . Czechoslovakia is a
new country. . . . Mussolini is raising 500,000 children every year and needs somewhere to stake 'em
out. . . . Portugal would like to join somebody in a
war. . . . Germany, the winner of the last war, is
about the only one not looking for trouble."

From London, Rogers wrote the following "cable"
to President Coolidge:

"Calcool, Washousewhite:

"Former Secretary of State Hughes had an interview with former Premier Briand of France, but
nothing official transpired, as neither carried an
employe's card. Russia wants to discuss debt payments with us. If you promise to pay America, it
will loan you twice as much as you promise to pay.
Wise guys, those Russians.

"Yours in exile, Willrog."

That Will Rogers' visits in foreign countries were
not all fun or his own pleasure was attested by the
late Ambassador Dwight W. Morrow, who admitted
he took Rogers to Mexico when relations between
that country and the United States needed "smooth-
ing out."

"I had my most satisfactory interview with President Calles after Rogers made him laugh," Morrow
declared.

Again after Rogers made his airplane flight over Nicaragua and contributed $50,000 for the earthquake sufferers, Secretary of State Stimson called him into conference on conditions there upon his return.

When Will was on his way to the Orient in 1931, he observed:

"Japan is going to hear the awfulest compliments, as I hear they don't stand for any wisecracks. Also, I don't speak their language and am having lots of trouble with my own."

One of his most quoted comments on politics had a word of praise for Mussolini:

"Mussolini could run this country with his eyes shut. In fact, that's the way our Congress has been running it."

On his return from one of his trips to London, he declared:

"I told 'em two weeks ago in London that the bankers there bet on their Government. Over here the bankers bet against it. The folks over there wouldn't think of going against England. It's a sort of patriotism."

Of the Peace Covenant he wrote:

"It says in there, 'There is to be no more war.' And there is a paragraph further down telling you where to get your ammunition in case there was one."

Another shrewd comment on international politics was made in New York at a luncheon shortly after the war, when he remarked:

"The only way to get ahead of Mr. Enright Commissioner of New York Police] is to walk in front of him.   Why, he even seems to have had business in Europe—he's the only official I know of who has been over there since the war on business.

"Secretary Hughes has been traveling and Secretary Denby and others—well, the new slogan, they tell me is: 'Join the Cabinet and see the world.' But what's the use?   You're sure to run into a war somewhere.

"My idea of stopping wars is to have nations act like individuals—if they don't like each other—move. Let France move to Japan and have Japan move to France.   Then if Japan and Germany got into a war, who would worry?   Why, America would run excursions to a war like that."

CHAPTER IX

ROGERS AND POLITICS

A S A COMMENTATOR on the ever-changing
political scene Will Rogers was the court jester
to the nation, but behind his straight-shooting
barbs of humor was a sound wisdom that was eagerly
sought by the high officials who were his targets.
The line from Shakespeare's *King Lear*: "Jesters
do oft prove prophets," was demonstrated as a
truism time and again by Rogers. Instead of
creating ill-feeling by his remarks, many felt honored
at being so noticed. It was related that a certain
United States Senator felt slighted because Rogers
had not included him in a radio speech in which he
lampooned Senator Borah.

"If you'd do as much for me as you did for Bill
Borah, I'd be famous," the slighted Senator complained.

Rogers had no political ambitions himself although
he was proposed for President several times. He
started his own presidental boom just as a joke in
1924, but four years later political observers were
considering the question seriously.

"Rogers is a statesman, experienced, courageous,
safe, and sound, and offers excellent material for
the Presidency," declared Representative Everett
B. Howard on the floor of Congress.

"Haw!" chuckled Rogers. "Do you want a President who is funny on purpose? A comedian can only last until he takes himself serious or his audience takes him serious, and I don't want either of those to happen to me, so let's stop all this foolishness right now."

A few days later in an article in *The Saturday Evening Post,* he formally withdrew as a candidate. He further suggested that Governor Alfred E. Smith decline the 1928 nomination of the Democratic party and wait to run four years later. He predicted then that the Democrats would win by a large majority in 1932. Political experts later declared that had Smith accepted Rogers' advice, he might have followed President Hoover.

After Herbert Hoover was nominated by the Republican party and Governor Smith by the Democrats, Rogers invented the Bunkless party with himself as the candidate for President.

"I want it understood first off that my platform is made out of the planks carried in by voters. Anybody with ten votes can have a plank. We are leaving room between planks for any wisecracks that we think should be inserted. We also will not only give the farmer relief: we'll cure him of being a farmer."

FAMOUS ELECTION BROADCAST

At the Friars Club in New York on the eve of the 1928 election, Rogers listened to his brother members telling how Friar Al Smith could not possibly lose the following day.

"I like Al Smith," Rogers drawled, "but you fellows are going to wake up tomorrow and find there is a big country west of the Hudson River."

One of his most famous satires on politics was delivered during a radio broadcast over the Columbia network on November 11, 1934. He said:

"Well, this is the last night you're going to be pestered with me for a while. I'm off for five Sundays, but in six weeks from tonight, why—git ready to tune me out.

"I got a lot of countries I want to talk to you about later on this winter. I've been written a thousand letters about Russia and all these other places, and asked lots of questions that I haven't been able to answer, and I wanted to talk—I wanted to do a little bit on it tonight, but something has happened that made me kind of alter my whole program for tonight.

"A friend passed away since I talked with you last Sunday night, and I wouldn't feel right if I— well, if I didn't change my program to say a few words about him. Well, I can't be eloquent and I can't be worthy of doing it, but I'm going to try and make up in sincerity and feeling what I lack in words.

"When you've heard of somebody since child- hood—well then, as you grew up and met him and come to know him and to like him, and see him become almost a tradition—then see him pass out right when it should have been the most useful years of his life. I don't know, it kind of gits me. He'd been ill, but he was feeling more hopeful.

But last Tuesday morning about seven he started
having acute pains, and as the day went on, they
got worse.   They called in what little medical
help they had, but it was feared he was beyond
human aid, and by nightfall—just as the sun was
setting—he breathed his last, this gallant old figure
who had been loved by many, feared by many,
had gone to where there's no returning.   All that
was mortal of the Republican party had left this
earth.

"Don't applaud.   Don't applaud, boys.   They're
dying.   He passed away—he passed away because
he wanted to live like a pioneer.   He couldn't
change with modern civilization.   The word spread
like wildfire.   The news was flashed to the four
corners of our land, from the nostrils of every
static radio belched forth the news, 'The King is
dead—the King is dead.'

"It struck us like a thunderbolt.   We knew that
he was ill.   We knew that he had really never recovered from that stroke which he had in October
of 1929.   A paralytic stroke brought on by a loss
of marginal blood.   That stroke laid him low, and
it happened just when he was at the height of his
career—just when things looked the brightest for
him—just when he was bragging of being rugged
—Oh, so rugged.   Why, there was not a dark
cloud that he could see on his horizon.   He was
made practically bedridden.   It was the unexpected that struck him and his immediate family.
He'd been warned, but not by any of his own
doctors or close friends.   But he'd been warned

by outsiders that he was living a little too high,
and it was liable to bring on a fluttering heart.

"But he scoffed at 'em: 'What do they know
about me and my health!   They're just jealous of
my ruddy condition.   They can't match my power,
and they're envious.   I'll keep on living like this
forever.   I've solved the problem of power—mass
energy.   Ah, that's it—mass energy, and we've
solved it.'   And then came the dawn.

"But just give the old boy credit.   When the
blow hit him, he was bright right up to the finish.
He was bright.   In October in '29 with no climatic
warning, he lived up to all political—he lived right
up to it—all political tradition.   He said 'it wasn't
my fault.'

"And it wasn't his fault.   It was everybody's
fault.   It was your fault—it was my fault—it was
the Lord's fault.   He just stepped in and said—
wait a minute.   How long has this thing been going
on here—this living on dog-eat-dog principle?
We'll stop this thing right here now, and give the
folks a chance to reorganize and redeem yourselves.
That's what the Lord told him.

"Now here's where the mistake was made.   The
Republicans held a clinic at that very moment and
decided: 'Boys, our patient is sick.   He's got acute
appendicitis.   Now, of course, an operation is
going to cost us all something, and we're all going
to have to chip in.   It will take part of what we
have, but it may save us in the long run.   There's
a change coming in our lives, and we can't do the
things we've always done.   We can no more ask

for the same conditions to continue than we can ask for our youth to continue.'

"Now had that been done, why this obituary notice that was posted on every crossroad last Tuesday night might not have been put there. But instead they decided to—at the clinic—that it really wasn't appendicitis at all—that it was just cramp colic. And that a strong, healthy man like he was—he could just throw it off, you know. He'd always been healthy and there was no reason he should be sick, and the only thing to do was just to let nature take its course, that they had always come out of these cramp colics without having to give up anything, and there was no reason why this one should be any different.

"As I say, from October, 1929, to November the 4th, 1932—get that date—November the 4th, 1932— on that date nature took its course again. The patient had another stroke, and they still said they wouldn't have to operate. They rushed with the ice bags again but not with a knife. They still contended that they was right, and the disease was wrong. Well, in an argument with a disease, be it physical or economical, you'd better give—you'd better give 'em a hearing anyhow.

"But in spite of all his pain—in spite of all his groans—the doctors and his whole family maintained he was fundamentally sound; that he had never been operated on in his life, and had lived this long, and that they could see no reason to think that this same life program and schedule should not go on as it always had.

"So he had his third and last stroke last Tuesday. He went to his maker a physical wreck but fundamentally sound. And on his tombstone—and on his tombstone it says: 'Here lies a rugged individual, but he wasn't rugged enough to compete with the Democrats.'

"Now we come to that grave question—that grave question of reincarnation. Does the soul return in another body? I believe it does. I don't know much about it, but I really believe that it returns, in another body. I don't know what animal he'll come back in. It won't be as big as an elephant, I know that. It will be—it will be something with much less humility. It will be a domestic animal—some very domestic animal. An animal more in the nature of a dog. It will have faith. Its whole soul will be consecrated to service. Will this animal be needed? It certainly will be, for the Democrats by that time will have passed out through too much power. The Democrats could never stand power as long as the Republicans could, because they never was used to it. They're getting cocky already, and they've only been in there overnight.

"So the Republicans being the first to die, they'll be the first to come back. So let's say a good word for the deceased, and tell him to be ready to move over in his grave—the Democrats will be crawling in there with him pretty soon."

'ALFALFA BILL" INDORSES ROGERS

In the 1932 Democratic National Convention at Chicago, "Alfalfa Bill" Murray, former Governor of

Oklahoma, startled the gathering when on the second vote he threw Oklahoma's twenty-two votes to Will Rogers. The cowboy philosopher, who had entered upon the political stage of the country through the back door of criticism, did not take the shift in his direction very seriously. As a matter of fact, when the votes were recorded for him, he was peacefully dozing in the press box. Politicians and the public thought that "Bill" Murray was indulging in another of his practical jokes. Some even expressed the opinion that Rogers was not the only "gag man" that Oklahoma produced.

Yet Murray was serious. He was convinced that Will Rogers would have made a great President and a popular one. Murray and Rogers had been friends for years, and the former Governor knew Will's father when the two had served on the Constitutional Convention at the admission of Indian Territory into the Union as the State of Oklahoma.

"The world never knew Rogers' great depth of character and intellect," Murray declared. "I regarded him not as the country's foremost humorist but rather as a clear thinker, a man of rare wisdom and a born statesman."

Political observers credited Rogers with being largely responsible for causing California to vote in the Democratic column for Franklin D. Roosevelt that year. Normally, California went Republican by two and three to one. Rogers' influence was exerted when Roosevelt and his campaign party were about to visit Los Angeles, where he was scheduled for one of the most important speeches of the campaign. Mayor John Porter was a Republican and he declared that he would not welcome in an official capacity a candidate who believed in the repeal of prohibition. Roosevelt backers feared Porter's decision would be detrimental to their nominee and they were in a quandary. Rogers, a lifelong Democrat, heard of the difficulty and offered to make the welcoming speech. The Roosevelt rally was held in the Coliseum and every one of the 100,000 seats in the place was sold at prices ranging from one to five dollars each. Rogers himself bought $1,800 worth of tickets and gave them away to stenographers, stage hands, and extras on the movie lot. The night of the rally, Rogers was never in better form, and of course his principal target was Mayor Porter. He bombarded the Republicans with good-natured barbs of humor and the gathering proved to be the turning point in the campaign in California. When the final returns were counted, it was found that Mayor Porter's action had turned into a boomerang and California had gone Democrat for the first time in sixteen years.

POLITICS ROGERS' TARGET

On the movie lot at Movietone City, fellow actors used to say that when Will Rogers met anyone for the first time he would ask whether the visitor was a Democrat or a Republican. It was said that he put this question to a famous, wealthy Easterner who had sought an introduction to Rogers.

"Republican," replied the Easterner.

"Shucks, that's too bad," Will is reported to have said.   "Well, see you tomorrow."

The last part of the humorist's remarks, according to the legend, was delivered over Rogers' shoulder as he walked away from the astounded visitor.

John J. Raskob, former National chairman of the Democratic party, however, was brought out to the Rogers' ranch for a visit when he arrived on the Pacific coast.   One morning, Will routed him out of bed and brought the great industrialist down to the corral where Rogers put on a thrilling exhibition of roping, bulldogging, and tying steers.

"The best way to hogtie an ornery steer quick is to pretend he is a Republican," Rogers told Raskob.

Then before Raskob could catch his breath from laughter, Rogers sent over the following like the crack of a bull whip:

"Darned if I don't think most of them are!"

The Democrats, however, did not escape and he found much in the New Deal of President Roosevelt to criticize in his gentle fashion.   Congress was his favorite target at all times.

"Now this is a very momentous Congress that is in session now," Will said a few months before his death.   "Mr. Roosevelt is trying to get rid of them. They have appropriated more money than any Congress ever did, but I guess that's all right. We are not paying our national debt, anyhow, so it don't matter how much it is, anyway."

Senator Huey P. Long, the filibustering Democrat from Louisiana, who died from an assassin's bullet, more than once provided Rogers with material for a witticism. Commenting on the night the "Kingfish" conducted his all-night filibuster in the Senate, Rogers said:

"At that he pulled the biggest and most educational novelty ever introduced in the Senate. He read the Constitution of the United States. A lot of 'em thought he was reviewing a new book."

During Roosevelt's campaign in 1932 the phrase "the forgotten man" was coined and used until it became threadbare. When Roosevelt announced the personnel of his Cabinet, most of them were names new to National affairs, which caused Rogers to remark:

"Scurrying through *Who's Who*, the *World Almanac*, and the United States Fingerprint Department trying to find out who they were, I can say the forgotten man has been found. There's nine of 'em and a woman."

William Jennings Bryan, "The Great Commoner," who made three unsuccessful bids for President on the Democratic ticket, felt the force of Will's barbed shafts during a Democratic National Convention to which both had been assigned as special writers. While seated in the section reserved for the press, Rogers kept up a steady stream of humorous comment. The reporters, bent on getting their copy into the newspapers on time, were sometimes annoyed, but in spite of themselves they frequently had to stop and laugh at Rogers' remarks.

Something Rogers said or wrote irritated the pompous Bryan and he took occasion to call Rogers' attention to it.

"I am a humorous writer," said Will, apparently very humble but with a suspicious twinkle in his eye.

Bryan drew himself up stiffly and replied, "I am a serious writer."

"Maybe we are both wrong," countered Rogers.

RIDICULES AMERICAN POLITICS

Will could always be depended upon to point out the ridiculous in the American political scene, as was evidenced on the occasion when a Senator arose to read into the *Congressional Record* one of Rogers' comments. Another Senator objected to the procedure.

"This other Senator rose and said, does the gentleman yield?" declared Will. "They always call each other gentlemen in there. By the tone they put in the word it would be more appropriate if they come right out and said, 'does the coyote from Maine yield?' Then the man from Maine says, 'I yield,' for if he don't, the other guy keeps on talking anyhow. So the coyote from Maine says, 'I yield to the polecat from Oregon.'

"So when all the yielding and objections is over, the other Senator said, 'I object to the remarks of a professional joker being put into the *Congressional Record.*' Taking a dig at me, see? They didn't want any outside fellow contributing. Well, he had me wrong. Compared to them I'm an amateur, and the thing about my jokes is that they don't hurt anybody. You can say they're not funny or they're terrible or they're good or whatever it is, but they don't do no harm.

"But with Congress—every time they make a joke it's a law. And every time they make a law it's a joke."

But more than one politician attested that Rogers had counseled and aided them through his writings and speeches. At a dinner before the exclusive Gridiron Club in Washington, Eddie Cantor related that a prominent statesman described Rogers as "America's policeman."

"He is without doubt the most potent individual influence in our national affairs," the statesman told Cantor, "and that goes for the President, the Cabinet, and the financiers who are supposed to wield such an influence over legislation.

"Congressmen have found out through bitter experience that their constituents pay more attention to what Will Rogers says in that little daily newspaper box than to a decision of the Supreme Court. A few adverse words from Rogers means sure death for any piece of legislation."

But of Congress, Will said:

"There is no credit to being a comedian, when you have the whole Government working for you. All you have to do is report the facts. I don't even have to exaggerate."

PRESIDENTS ENJOY JOKES

Rogers began "kidding" Presidents during the Wilson Administration just before the United States entered the World War. Rogers was starring in a show and President Wilson went from Washington to Baltimore to see it when it played in that city.

Trouble was brewing on the Mexican border and the punitive expedition of the United States had failed in its attempt to capture the Mexican rebel leader, Pancho Villa. Criticism was being hurled from all sides at the Government for the unpreparedness of the Army.

"There is some talk of getting a machine gun if we can borrow one," said Rogers, spinning his lariat and looking over at President Wilson. "The one we have now they are using to train our army at Plattsburg. If we go to war, we'll just have to go to the trouble of getting another gun."

President Wilson, who found his chief recreation in attending vaudeville and musical comedies, laughed heartily at Rogers, and the comedian realized that the erudite head of the Nation could take a joke in the spirit in which it was intended.

"President Wilson," continued Rogers, "is getting along fine now to what he was a few months ago. Do you realize, people, that at one time in our negotiations with Germany he was five notes behind?"

The President never laughed more uproariously at a joke, and the theater went wild. It was something new in the experience of theatergoers to have a President join in the fun. It was one of the most successful nights that Rogers ever enjoyed on the stage.

OVERNIGHT GUEST AT WHITE HOUSE

In October, 1926, after Rogers had returned from abroad where he wrote that series of side-splitting *Letters of a Self-made Diplomat to His President,*

President Coolidge wired an invitation to him to visit the White House as an overnight guest. Rogers was overwhelmed.

"If it's a joke," Rogers wired in reply, "head me off at Philadelphia."

It was no joke, however, and Coolidge sat up until late at night talking to Rogers.

"I am the only Democrat who has slept in the White House for a long time," said Rogers in describing the visit. "Of course, the President's not understood. He's a nice fellow with a sense of humor. We spent last night swapping yarns. About eight o'clock the President began to yawn and at ten he fell asleep on me."

Coolidge was responsible for many of Rogers' jests, but one of the best stories of the two men was prompted by Will's bosom companion, Irvin S. Cobb, the famous writer. The two were about to meet Coolidge for the first time, and the President's solemnity on all occasions caused Cobb to remark, "I'll bet you can't make him smile."

As the President shook hands with Rogers, he said something through his tight lips. Will leaned over as though to hear better, and said:

"Pardon me. I didn't get the name."

The President smiled.

When Coolidge quit the White House after his term in office had expired and went back to live in a modest double house in Northampton, Massachusetts, Rogers paid tribute to him in this manner:

"There was evidence of the real American. No fuss, no crowds. Can't you picture it? A man going from the White House to a smaller abode where he hands out $47.50 rent. That was the most remarkable part of his administration. He was able to find a house at that rent."

Rogers used to tell of a Gridiron Dinner that he attended at Washington where the table was so big that President Hoover at one end of it was in the District of Columbia and he was at the other end in the State of Virginia.

"They lined up the ambassadors near President Hoover," he would relate, in the manner of one imparting a state secret. "They were seated according to how much they owed Uncle Sam. The ones that owed the most sat near the President. Down at my end of the table were the South American ambassadors. They couldn't see or hear much and they grumbled. I tipped them off to get their countries to borrow a few billions from us."

The social war that raged in Hoover's Administration over the place Mrs. Dolly Gann, sister of Vice President Curtis, should occupy at Presidential functions was described by Rogers as "a scrap over who should sit next to the President." Curtis' job, he said, was to bang the gavel for "the opening of the Senate with a prayer and closing with an investigation."

At the 1932 Democratic National Convention, Will Rogers was as prominent as Al Smith and Franklin D. Roosevelt. Eddie Dowling, musical comedy star, introduced his old friend to the convention, and for fifteen minutes the Smith and Roosevelt factions forgot their differences as they roared at Will's jibes at the leaders of the Democratic party.

Every morning at the convention he would go over to the Oklahoma delegation and greet them. The group occupied seats in front of the press box. Among the delegates were several close friends.

"Good morning, you old coyotes," he would shout in a voice that could be heard all over the hall. "If ever there was a delegation that was a disgrace to a state, it's you bunch of boys. See that you behave yourselves today."

The delegation would reply with some similar "insult," and Rogers would laugh heartily as he walked away.

As great as his affection obviously was for Al Smith, Rogers was extremely fond of President Roosevelt and he delighted in telling of a visit to the White House and found the President laughing uproariously. The President, he said, was sitting in bed at the time with newspapers around him.

"He was laughing," Will said, "at what the papers said about him."

POKES FUN AT ADMINISTRATION

But Roosevelt's policies did not escape unscathed from his piercing barbs. When the United States went off the gold standard, Roosevelt, according to reports, was very much annoyed when Rogers described the Supreme Court as "the nine old men in kimonos," who were going to force the Democrats to return the forty-one cents they had taken from the Republican dollar.

Another poke at Roosevelt and his "Brain Trust" was contained in his argument that the farm problem might be solved "If every farmer would eat all that he raised; then he would not only get fat himself but farm products might probably go up.

" 'Course, on account of this not being an economist's idea," he continued, "it might not work."

Rogers was a lifelong Democrat but he studiously avoided partisanship. He contributed to the Democratic campaign funds, but at the same time he frequently appeared on benefit programs to raise money for the Republican treasury. Republican leaders sought his counsel in their campaigns as often as did the Democrats. Of his own political affiliation, he once said, "I am not a member of any organized party—I am a Democrat."

MAYOR OF BEVERLY HILLS

Will Rogers once was known as the "Mayor of Beverly Hills" but the fact of the matter was that he never was anything more than "honorary Mayor." It was all a joke, and for two years he pretended he was a political boss of the moving-picture colony.

He took the "oath of office" on December 2, 1926, after Douglas Fairbanks had made the introductory speech. The Los Angeles Fire Department Band played "The Old Gray Mare" and Will made his "inaugural address" while the throng roared with laughter.

"I am for the common people," he declared, "and as Beverly Hills has no common people, I'll be sure to make good."

He promised to see that the "poor" of the city would be given bigger and better private swimming pools and miles of new bridle paths on which to canter to work up an appetite for breakfast.

His constituents later complained that as "Mayor" he spent very little time in town.

"I confess," he replied. "I've been running around the country exhibiting myself. And I'll tell you the answer. I am God's gift to those who didn't see Queen Marie."

CHAPTER X

ROGERS THE PHILANTHROPIST

WILL ROGERS was a philanthropist whom any man might well emulate. From the day that he used his last cent to pay the homeward passage of his homesick companion from the Argentine and faced the world with empty pockets, Will always had a ready hand for the needy. In the days when he was an impecunious rider and roper in Wild West shows, he was known for his eagerness to share what he had with someone less fortunate. As he climbed along the path to glory, his generosity kept pace with his mounting earnings. He gave without any ostentation, invariably masking his good deed in anonymity. No one, not even Rogers himself, could estimate the money he gave away. It was easily a good-sized fortune even viewed by the standards of wealthy men of his time. He gave without question and once when friends warned him that a certain man to whom he had given money was a fraud, Will only grinned and replied: "The poor devil probably needs it worse than I do." Everything he touched turned into money, but he worked for it and earned every penny of the huge amounts that came streaming in from the moving pictures, his writings, and broadcasts over the radio. In return for his good fortune he made the burden lighter for thousands not only in the United States but far beyond its confines. The greatest word in the life of Will Rogers was *Charity*. He had a myriad of definitions for it and used every one of them. His public charities were legion but his private charities would make even a longer roll.

"MONEY DOESN'T WORRY ME"

Money to Rogers meant only the means of doing greater good for his fellow man. He never sought it for himself and, after he had provided security for his beloved family, he once remarked while in a serious mood: "Money doesn't worry me any more. All I care about is a good blue suit." He paused a second and went on: "It doesn't even have to be good."

Many old actors and vaudeville players, friends of his leaner days, found him a sure haven of refuge when hard times overtook them and there were no "bookings" to bring them in a livelihood.

Walter Kelly, famous "Virginia Judge" of the stage, screen, and radio, told of an old actor he had known who was spending his declining days in California. A group of New York actors had dug down into their "grouch bags" and raised enough money to send the old man to the coast, in the hope that he might eke out a living playing small parts in the movies. He failed to connect.

"I met him in a bank one day," Kelly said, "and asked him whether he was putting in money or taking it out. He showed me a check of $25 signed by Will Rogers.

" 'I'm putting it in,' the old fellow replied. 'I get one every week. It's what keeps me off the relief rolls. A lot of others get one like it each week, here and in New York. Will Rogers is taking care of us.' "

There must have been an army of persons that Will "took care of" as the incident related by Bernard Granville, popular musical comedy star, who was associated with Rogers in vaudeville, will show. It took place in St. Louis.

"One morning he left the hotel early," Granville related. "I followed, thinking we might have some fun together. He headed rapidly down the street and into a poor neighborhood. When I caught up with him, he was pressing money into the hand of a poor, aged woman who had been dispossessed, and was sitting forlornly amidst her belongings in the street. How he heard of her case, I do not know.

"When Rogers saw me, he was acutely embarrassed.

" 'Bernard,' he pleaded, 'don't tell this around. They will just think it was a publicity stunt, and it wasn't.' "

Granville kept it secret for twenty-five years, only telling of it after Rogers died.

Whatever theater Rogers happened to be playing in, turned out to be the Mecca of stage folk that had known better times. It made no difference whether he had ever played with them or not.

An old Shakespearean actor, who might have been mistaken for the Melancholy Dane in person, gained admittance to Rogers' dressing room one day. The actor showed Rogers a lot of old programs—relics of the days when he had appeared with great stars.

"And here I am, one of the old stars, broke," declared the tragedian.

Will laughed as the old actor awaited the effect of his plea.

"Well, old timer," said Rogers, "it looks like you saved programs instead of money."

With the comment, however, Rogers' hand went down into his pocket and he gave the old player enough to carry him over for a month at least.

A FRIEND OF COWBOYS

Cowboys, or men who said they once were cowboys and had ridden with Rogers in Wild West shows, were always asking aid from Rogers. Many of them were probably nothing better than panhandlers and had no claim on him but he never questioned their pleas.

While making the motion picture *Steamboat Round the Bend*, however, he heard of an old cowboy with whom he actually worked in a Wild West show. The former friend would not go to Rogers, however, because he felt that the Oklahoman was too big a man to be bothered. Rogers left the movie lot one afternoon and went to see his old fellow rider. It was after midnight before he returned.

Charles Dillingham, manager-producer, gave a comprehensive picture of the hard-working Will and his picturesque generosity. Dillingham said:

"He was just like all other critics. He could tear other people to pieces, but let anyone criticize him and he was grief stricken. His industry entitled him to the place of critic. He was the hardest working person I knew. During the long run of *Three Cheers* he had a suite in the Hotel Astor just below mine, but I never saw him around. Nor did anyone else. This puzzled me.

" 'Where can he be?' I asked myself time and again.

"Then one day by chance, I found that he was in the theater at nine in the morning. He worked constantly until noon, then stole across the way and had a bite of lunch; then came back and worked again until dinner time. And even then, not content, he would often be back at work long before the evening performance began and long before anyone else in the theater was around. You see, he had discovered that the theater was the best place for him to work. There was no telephone there and no chance of meeting scores of people who are continually molesting celebrities—seeking interviews, introductions, miscellaneous favors. He had his typewriter next his make-up box and such books and papers as he needed, and his great energy kept him working continuously and happily at the many tasks he has assigned for himself.

"This studious isolation did not, however, crowd out his human side. He always found time for charity. Will Rogers' dislike of making charities public was honest and thorough. Sometimes he would be at the stage door in earnest conversation with people from back home. To be sure, he never knew them out there and never knew of their existence until they appeared suddenly before him, urgent and needy. This did not prevent him from gruffly handing them money for their night's lodging and telling them to be sure to go to a good hotel.

"He had a habit also of going to the box office and getting ten- and twenty-dollar bills changed to one-dollar bills. Then equipped with a wad of these, he strolled down the street. Curious about his intentions, I followed him one day and learned what he did with the money. It all went, dollar bill by dollar bill, to friends of former days—old timers with whom he had played on the small vaudeville circuits when he was a beginner—poor also and unknown.

" 'Will, give me a nickel for a cup of coffee,' someone would say to him.

"Rogers would stuff a bill into the petitioning hand—then another dollar into another hand—and then he would make his way homeward."

CANTOR BUYS STOCK FOR ROGERS

Eddie Cantor once had an experience with Rogers' generosity, although for a time Eddie had some misgivings about the whole affair. Cantor had what he considered a very good "tip" on a certain Trust Company stock. He met Rogers and advised the Oklahoman to invest some money in it right away. Rogers, who believed only in investing his money in real estate and insurance, told Cantor: "I don't know anything about the stock market, Eddie."

"You don't have to know anything about it, Bill," Cantor replied. "It's bound to go up. I am sure of it.   I'll buy a block of it for you and then we can fix up the money later."

"If you say it's all right, Eddie, go ahead."

Cantor bought the stock in Rogers' name and Will went on the road on his "lecture" tour.   The stock climbed steadily until it was nearly twenty points above the purchase price.   Then came a slight reaction in the market and the stock dropped off two points.   Cantor received a long-distance telephone call from Detroit.   It was Rogers, insisting that Cantor sell the stock at once.   Cantor tried to argue with Rogers to hold it for a while longer but it was no use.

Eddie was angry because Rogers had not put up any money but he sold the stock and a check for $6,200, the profit on transaction, was sent to Will.   In the return mail from Detroit was a letter from Rogers.

In it was the check, indorsed by Rogers and made payable to Cantor's "fresh-air" camp for poor boys.

SALVATION ARMY A PET CHARITY

Another boys' camp in which Rogers had more than a passing interest was the Shag Bark Camp of the Salvation Army in Kenosha County, Wisconsin. The Army was one of Will's pet charities and in 1933 he gave $10,000 to build the camp.   He also provided funds to send 225 music students and 150 Boy Scouts to the camp in 1935.

When working on a picture, Rogers always would find out in advance the number of days allotted for its completion.   If, as often happened, the production was finished ahead of schedule, he'd get a copy of the payroll from the assistant director and pay the wages of everyone in the company with the exception of featured players, the director, and others on high salary for the full time.

"Scmetimes it's a long time between pictures for these folks," he would explain, "and they need all they can get. I'd hate to think by speedin' up a bit I'd cheated anybody outa their groceries."

When a friend once spoke disparagingly of the community chest and said that most of those receiving help didn't deserve it, Will made a characteristic remark which summed up his whole theory of giving:

"What of it?" he demanded. "They're human, ain't they? An' they gotta eat just the same as you and me."

It was not in money alone that Rogers revealed his charity. The story is told of the time when he was the featured star in the Ziegfeld Follies in 1924 at the New Amsterdam Theater, New York. Will was living out on Long Island and used the train to the Pennsylvania Station every night in time to reach the theater for the show. One night as he was hurrying from the train he noticed a young mother overburdened with children and baggage.

Rogers noticed the young, poorly dressed woman with an infant asleep in her arms, a sleepy child of about three years old beside her, and several large parcels. He stopped while the rest of the passengers left the train. Then he took the older child by the hand, gathered up the bundles under his free arm, and led the young woman up the stairs to the waiting room. There he found her a seat, deposited her parcels, tipped his hat, and smiled. That duty performed, Rogers rushed away so that he would not be late at the theater. Will thought no one saw that kindly act, but a neighbor who witnessed the incident told of it after Rogers had passed into the great beyond.

DONATED SERVICES TO BENEFITS

Rogers could not resist any appeal for aid. While he was starring on Broadway he was continually being led from one benefit performance to another. He always donated his services and the benefit promoters showed him no mercy. When he wasn't on the stage, he was speeding from one place to another in a taxicab. Sometimes he did not know what the benefit was all about.

"Along about the seventh appearance before a different audience one night, I became kinder curious," Rogers said. "I tried to find out, and as near as I could gather it was for the benefit of the poor golf players of Great Neck."

Will at the time was living in Great Neck, Long Island, but he never took up the ancient Scottish game.

During Christmas week in 1922, he appeared at a number of charity affairs, and one night it was in the early hours before he was finished. "I think I'll knock off and call it a day," he declared.

It was only about seven hours later, however, that he was performing on top of a bus in the Fifth Avenue parade of the Friars' Flying Circus raising Christmas funds for destitute children.

"I didn't get no time to buy a Christmas present for the wife," he lamented, "but I sent her a few dollars to buy some food for our own kids."

IN FRONT RANK AS HUMORIST

In a sense, it was Rogers' charity work that placed him in the front rank as a humorist. During the World War in 1917, Winfield Sheehan, later to be his boss in the talking pictures, was named captain of the stage-screen fund team of the Red Cross. The theatrical team raised over $2,000,000 along Broadway and Rogers played a prominent part in getting the money. Will at the time was drawing $750 a week for playing in the Follies, and $250 a week for the Midnight Frolic. Rogers strolled into the Red Cross headquarters and donated $1,000 in cash. He then signed a pledge to donate one tenth of his salary for the duration of the war. Then, as casually as he strolled in, he turned around and walked out.

Sheehan, however, heard of it and sought Rogers out as a member of his team. He took Rogers to a luncheon meeting of the New York Chamber of Commerce where the teams reported daily. Rogers made the report for the stage-screen workers and at the same time delivered a speech that convulsed his audience with laughter. After the diners had roared at his witticisms, he suddenly turned serious and brought tears to their eyes. As he talked, he rubbed his own eyes with his coat sleeve. Some of New York's wealthiest men were in that audience and the contributions that day made a record for the drive.

From then on, the star of the Red Cross campaign was Rogers. Word of his humor spread among the workers and they thronged the luncheon meetings to hear him. As a result, those who had never seen him in the theater went there and his fame spread quickly, not only in New York but all over the country. As the years went by, he could always be depended upon to go campaigning for the Red Cross, and he raised substantial sums for the organization. After he became prosperous, he always started his work with his own donation, which was never less than $10,000. He was elected a life member of the Red Cross in 1927, after his great campaign in raising funds for the victims of Mississippi River flood. The lengthy Honor Roll of Rogers' work for the Red Cross was as follows:

McAlester, Okla., mine explosion, 1919, sixty-one men killed. Made large personal donation and raised generous fund for families of victims.

September, 1926. Worked with Charles Evans Hughes, later Chief Justice, in a Florida hurricane benefit aboard the *Leviathan*, raising $40,000 in a single performance.

Mississippi flood, 1927. By benefit personal appearances, raised more than $100,000 for flood sufferers.

January, 1931. Helped Red Cross organize nation-wide drought relief broadcast including President Hoover, former President Coolidge, and Al Smith.

Drought relief campaign of 1930–31. In airplane with Frank Hawks, speed flier, toured Midwest and

Far West, visiting several cities daily, and making speeches which greatly accelerated chapter giving.

Nicaraguan earthquake, 1931.   Flew to Nicaragua, gave $5,000 and cheer there, came back and raised a large Nicaraguan fund.

1933–34.   Donated $20,000 for continuing Red Cross public health nursing in places where it was to be cut off due to depression.   The Red Cross sent Rogers a pictorial report of the good done with this money.

May, 1933.   Rogers wired the Red Cross his intention of "litterin' up the mike with a little Oklahoma grammar" to "make contribution to a couple of good causes," unemployment relief work of the Red Cross and Salvation Army.

Rogers probably played more benefits for charity than any other star in the show business.   During Christmas week of 1934, he appeared at a dozen functions in the interest of the needy in and around Hollywood and Los Angeles.   In addition to appearing in person, he invariably gave the chairman a check for $100 or $200 before he left with admonition to "keep it quiet."

The Assistance League, an organization of women relatives of film-company officials that cares for the needy in the movie industry, always counted on a check for $100 every time he lunched in their restaurant.   It was one of his pet hobbies to take friends there who could afford it and then make them pay the check after first seeing that it was for a sizable amount.

ALWAYS READY TO LEND A HELPING HAND

Will Rogers was ever eager to extend a helping hand to anyone in other ways than by gifts of money. Joel McCrea, the movie star, told how Rogers aided him at a time when he was discouraged and about to abandon his career in the films. He met the genial Oklahoman on the movie lot one day just when the outlook seemed blackest.

"What's the matter, kid?" sang out Rogers. "You look like your last friend had busted into the bank, stole your life savings, and then eloped with your wife."

McCrea told Rogers the whole story and how he about decided to give up. Rogers listened patiently.

"Son," counseled Rogers, "what you need is to get some good dirt soil under your feet. Get yourself a piece of ground that you can call your own, a place where you can run away and hide and invite your soul to go along. Some place where you can get your perspective back. Plant something; grow something; raise something. Get some animals and then see how you like it."

McCrea bought a thousand-acre ranch in the San Fernando Valley, and Rogers advised him on the purchase of cattle, horses, and farming implements. Crops were planted and McCrea found life was not so drear as he thought. As his outlook changed, so did his luck. Success came his way as he was given better and better parts.

Will Rogers left an estate that was variously estimated. The exact amount was not made public, but it was generally believed that it was overestimated in press reports. A large portion of his fortune was invested in real-estate holdings in California and Oklahoma, in Government bonds, and in life insurance. His annual income came from motion pictures, his writings, and his radio broadcasts. Despite his open purse and ready hand, he was regarded by everyone with whom he had any dealings as a shrewd, but fair and reasonable business man. Ranked as one of the most successful of motion-picture stars, he also was among the few persons that carried life insurance of $250,000 or more. The bulk of his estate was bequeathed to his wife. His California real estate was considered valuable and included his ranch in the Santa Monica Canyon, a home in Beverly Hills, several ocean-front properties, and scattered holdings. A contract with the Fox Twentieth Century Film Company provided that he was to receive $200,000 a picture. Although film companies usually carried insurance on their stars to provide against accident and death, none was carried on Rogers, the biggest box-office attraction in the industry. That was due to Rogers' air activities, which made the insurance rate too high.

PROFESSIONAL vs. SOCIAL SERVICES

One story frequently told of Rogers revealed his shrewd business sense and at the same time his willingness to make those pay who could easily afford it. A California multi-millionaire sent Will a formal invitation to attend a dinner at his estate.

Rogers sent a formal acceptance and attended the dinner, where he was called upon to make a speech.

The next morning Rogers sent the wealthy man a bill for $1,000 for "professional services." A secretary of his host protested and said that Will had been asked in a purely social way.

"Oh, no," replied Rogers, "when people invite me alone, it's professional. When it's social, they include Mrs. Rogers and she wasn't invited."

The bill was paid. Rogers indorsed the check and donated it to charity.

There were countless anecdotes of Rogers dealing with checks he received and turned directly over to the Red Cross and the Salvation Army. In April, 1926, he appeared at a benefit of the United Jewish Campaign and matched the proceeds of the affair with his own check for $2,500. In Philadelphia, where he put on one of his first "one-man" shows for the benefit of the Charlotte Cushman Club, he charged $1,000 for his services. On receiving the money, he promptly turned it over to charity. So it went, wherever he was—Miami, New Orleans, Dallas, Hollywood, and scores of other places.

Mrs. Rogers, naturally, was proud of Will's extraordinary wit, but it was far more thrilling to her when he used that talent for the benefit of humanity. Shortly after their return from abroad in 1926, she revealed that she shared and encouraged him in going out of his way to perform some act of mercy.

"I am proudest of Will's humor," she said, "when it is used to help others in a material way. For instance, on this trip back from Europe, Will, with

others, raised more than $50,000 for sufferers in the
Miami hurricane.   It delighted me to think that
his humor and comedy could work together as such
a force for good.   Then I was pleased by another
act of thoughtfulness on his part.   One day while
in Europe, he read about the return of Miss Clara-
belle Barrett to the United States with a $2,000
debt hanging over her.   Miss Barrett had tried to
swim the English Channel.

" 'It's a shame that young woman,' Will said to
me, 'who made such a fine effort, should have financial worries added to her disappointment.'   The
young woman had already sailed for her home, so he
couldn't see her personally.   He sent a wireless to
Captain Hartley, on whose ship the girl had sailed,
and said he would give $500 to a fund.   He sug-
gested that Captain Hartley raise the other $1,500
on board.   The Captain did."

LOSS MOURNED BY CHARITABLE ORGANIZATIONS

No one knew how much money Rogers raised and
gave to his two pet charities, the Red Cross and the
Salvation Army, but the airplane tour made with
Frank Hawks on behalf of the Red Cross for the
drought sufferers brought in more than $275,000.
Rogers paid all the expenses of the trip and, outside
of the time he lost, he was $12,000 poorer at the end.

What Rogers meant to the Red Cross was expressed by James L. Fieser, acting chairman of the
national organization:

"Literally thousands of Red Cross chapter people
will personally miss Will Rogers," Fieser said, "not

only for his numerous gifts in the furtherance of better health, but on account of his encouragement to them as he often unexpectedly arrived at a point where need was greatest."

The Salvation Army voiced similar regret through Colonel William C. Arnold, chief secretary, who said:

"The tragic death of Will Rogers will be deeply lamented in Salvation Army circles. He was a long and practical friend of the organization. The proceeds of one of his radio broadcasts, amounting to $25,000, were handed over to General Evangeline Booth, who applied the gift to the promotion of summer camps for underprivileged boys and girls."

Puerto Rico recalled how Rogers had given a benefit performance for the victims of a hurricane there and years before had contributed generously to their milk fund.

Former President Cosgrave, of Ireland, brought to light the little-known fact that Will Rogers had given a benefit there on one of his numerous trips to Europe. Cosgrave said:

"He was a brave and intelligent man who kept strictly to the moral code in all his work. His charity was perhaps his outstanding feature. Years ago, when we had a very serious disaster at Brumcolligher, he came here specially to give a performance in Dublin to help collect a considerable sum for the relief of sufferers and contributed £100 himself.

"He was beloved by all who met him in Ireland and all were impressed with his great genius, humor, and genial treatment of every subject."

Will Rogers, a crack polo player, goes after the ball still high in the air at a game at Santa Monica.

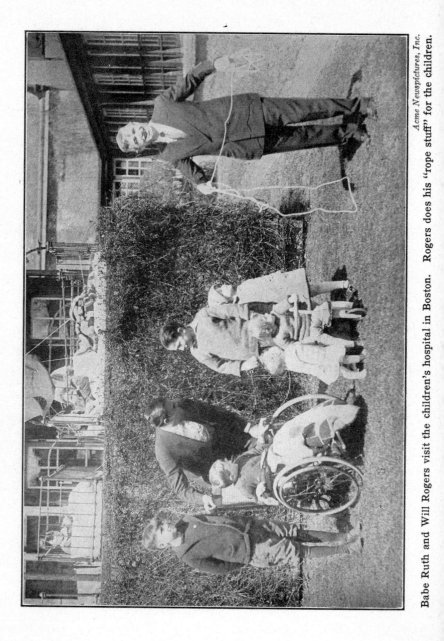

Babe Ruth and Will Rogers visit the children's hospital in Boston. Rogers does his "rope stuff" for the children.

ROGERS' BIG HEART

Wherever Rogers went, it was a signal for those in financial straits to rush forward with their hands extended—for a donation. In New York, it would be former actors, in California, ex-movie players, and in the cow country, one-time cowboys. Will was once sitting on the porch of a fashionable hotel in a health resort in the Southwest when an unshaven, dirty, bowlegged, old tramp came up to him.

"Don't you remember me, Will?" the little man said. "I used to ride with you in Zach Mulhall's show."

Rogers knew that if all the cowboys who claimed they had ridden with him in Wild-West outfits were enumerated, that branch of the show business would have had a larger census than the rest of the industry combined. He looked over the stranger and grinned.

"Old timer," Rogers drawled, "you don't look like you was a rider. You look like you been rode."

But the big heart of Rogers could not deny the man and he pressed a bill into the stranger's dirty fist.

As he summed it up, time and again: "I never hated anybody or anything."

CHAPTER XI

ON THE SPEAKER'S PLATFORM

WILL ROGERS violated every known rule of rhetoric and oratory but he was in demand everywhere as an after-dinner speaker, and fortunate was the diner who was present when he delivered one of his masterpieces. The lecture platform also proved his forte, and he laughingly referred to his "one-man shows," which sometimes ran hours beyond the time for closing, as "concerts."

"The greatest personal satisfaction I ever got was from my 'concerts,' Will once declared. "That was the hardest work but it was the most gratifying. Then you're out on the stage with no one to help you. The first season I used a quartet. The second season I was alone. People said you couldn't hold an audience two hours alone with no material but your own.

"But it worked and that's much more gratifying than playing in a picture—personally gratifying, I mean. After 'concerts' I'd put stage plays. The satisfaction the pictures give you is of covering a great territory almost without effort. Seems unbelievable that you make a picture and in no time at all it circles the globe.

"Talking once on the radio where there's no audience to see how your gags are going is harder than doing ten performances of a stage play or making a whole picture."

ON LECTURE TOUR

When the subject of going on a lecture tour was first broached to Rogers, he thought someone was trying to have some fun with him.   Charles L. Wagner, who conceived the idea, wrote to the humorist and offered a contract for $30,000 a month. Rogers paid no attention to it.

A week later Wagner was standing on Broadway with a friend when Will walked by.   Wagner told the friend how he had written to Rogers and received no reply.   Wagner's companion said he knew Rogers and volunteered to find out what the comedian thought of the lecture proposition.

"Well, I'll be darned," said Will, when he was asked about it.   "I received a letter like that, but I thought some of the boys at the Friars Club was kiddin' me.   You know, they gotta bartender up there named Charley Wagner."

He toured the United States under the direction of Wagner and "packed 'em in" night after night. He explained at every stop that he had no "message" and was not an "ambassador."   At New Orleans he was told of a plan to build a bridge over the mighty Mississippi River and he referred to it in his "concert."   The audience applauded but as the last handclap died away, he whipped over: "You told Mark Twain that, too."

Will was extremely proud of the fact that his lectures were given under all sorts of conditions.

"I had a clean show," he said, "and when we were booked into the church I didn't have to change a line of the patter—only had to cut out some of the rope stuff."

At Kansas City, on the eve of a Republican National Convention, he gave his "concert" for charity in a theater that filled to capacity two hours before he stepped out on the stage. Police had to be called out to control the great crowds outside that clamored to be admitted.

Joe Laurie, Jr., famous vaudeville and musical comedy star and a close friend of Will Rogers, told of meeting the comedian in Philadelphia where the humorist presented one of his lectures before an audience that included the most exclusive of the Quaker City's society. After the performance, Rogers declined all the invitations that were pressed upon him to visit the socially elect in their homes.

"Instead," Laurie related, "he came over to my hotel room and threw himself on the bed. The two of us talked until nearly four o'clock in the morning.

"He had just played in Oklahoma City a short time before, and he told me of the tremendous kick he got out of playing in his home State. The lecture was given in the Convention Hall and Rogers described how the people drove there in automobiles and mule carts."

Rogers started that show, Laurie continued, at 8.30 P. M. and finished at 11.30 P. M. but the people refused to go home, so he started in again and talked until 1.30 A. M.

"Tears came to his eyes," said Laurie, "when he told how a group of girls presented him with garlands of flowers and some old Indian women gave him a large, gaily-colored vase."

There were many stories told about Rogers refusing to wear a dinner coat at formal affairs but, according to Laurie, he blossomed out in a tuxedo the night the Friars Club gave a dinner to Will Hays, Judge Kenesaw Mountain Landis, and Augustus Thomas—the "three Czars" of motion pictures, baseball, and the stage, respectively. It was cut to resemble his blue suit, however, and he frequently joked about it.

"I'm getting to be like a fireman," he said. "Everytime I hear the word 'dinner' I slide into my dinner clothes, and dash off to attend it."

SPEECH AT FRIARS' CLUB A CLASSIC

It was as an after-dinner speaker that Will Rogers adopted an intimate type of address that he did not use at other places. The Friars were noted for the outstanding notables that graced their festive boards and whenever Rogers could get to New York, he was certain to be called upon to speak and he always "stole the show" away from the guest of honor. The night of the Hays-Landis-Thomas dinner he delivered the following classic:

"There is an awful lot of theatrical managers in the room tonight, and they know what it is, after years of experience, to miscast an act. If ever there was in the history of any theatrical dinners, or anything that anybody was miscast in, I'm him. I haven't even got the part dressed right. I don't have to tell you that I am out of place here. I have felt it more than you do out there, because I knew that I didn't belong. I worked over at our club, at the Friars, at a few little bush league dinners that we have had and that was all right, that was over there, we were feeding people that really needed it.

"But I came over here tonight, in this big league affair, and I knew that I didn't belong. All of my friends sitting around here will tell you that, during the entire evening, I was afraid to eat. I was hungry, I admit that. Actors usually are—but I couldn't eat, because I knew that when I got up to speak I would be liable to boot one. The point I am trying to make is that I didn't eat here tonight and, if I am rotten, I don't owe you anything.

"They told me: 'Will, we are going to give a big dinner and we are going to entertain the three biggest men of the three biggest amusement industries in the world, and we have conferred quite an honor on you. We are going to let you in and you are going to speak on the man that represents the biggest industry.

"I started in to work, I read everything that I could get pertaining to it, but I didn't ask who the man was, because it didn't make any difference to me who he was—the industry which he represented was so vast that it dwarfed the man and it didn't make any difference who he was, I didn't care, it was what he represented, and I didn't even ask.

"I brought to this hotel here tonight, a fifteen-
or a twenty-minute speech—fifteen without laughs,
and twenty with laughs. As I came in from the
outside there, I met one of these gentlemen, and he
says to me 'I see, Will, that you are going to give us
some stuff on Hays.'

"I said, 'What Hays?' and he said, 'Will Hays,
he is the man, Will Hays of the movies.'

"Well, sir, I give you my word that in all of my
little career in New York here, since I arrived with
that carpet bag I was never more upset, because
you could have knocked me out with a feather.
There, I had gone two whole weeks, after they told
me that it was the biggest amusement business in
the world—I had gone home and I had prepared this
address on bootlegging.

JIBES AT THE MOVIE INDUSTRY

"I am going to admit to you folks that, with all
of my little experience of the stage, I was stuck, and
I am stuck yet because, in comparison, you know that
I got all of this stuff on a wonderful industry, and
then to find that you have got to drop right down to
moving pictures! Well, it is a terrible setback, you
know, to have to come down from a national commodity and talk about a ten-cent serial—why even
cornflakes, which is the lowest form of cereal in the
world, and they sell for twenty cents. And just
think that I have to come here and tell you about
this ten-cent industry—it is not fair, because you
know bootlegging is an honor. There is something
to it. It means something. You are selling a staple

article, something that is good today. But what are the movies? Only a lot of storms with different names to them. You can't do that, that don't go.

"The movies is something that is made for children, while bootlegging is made for men—you know it means something. I am really handicapped here tonight, because now, you take the liquor industry with one man—why, if he takes two drinks of Scotch, or something like that, two drinks of Scotch commands more respect than all of the hair oil of a Valentino, or the toothpaste of a Fairbanks. You would consider a successful hootch man of more reputation than all the Blood and Sand and Robin Hoods combined. But getting right down to it, take just one quart of Scotch that has been sent to this country by way of Canada, and it has been diluted and sold and resold in more towns than Chaplin has been 'The Kid' in, and it is unfair to ask a man to defend an industry that winds around and around and gets nowhere.

"But then you say, that is all right, you are not supposed to talk about the industry. What you are supposed to talk about is the man that represents the industry. Well, there he is—just look at him, that little bird—what are you going to say about him—I don't know! I have known him for years and on account of that I shouldn't have been asked to speak for him. From now on I will have to make up my stuff as I go along, and it is almost as hard to think about something I can say about him as it is about the industry he represents. There is just one thing that is a good sign tonight about this dinner.

Will Rogers with Henry Ford and his son, Edsel, enjoying the opening World Series game at Detroit.

Franklin D. Roosevelt, James Roosevelt, Senator McAdoo, and Chairman James A. Farley, enjoying Rogers' humor at the Democratic Convention in Chicago.

When I found that I am to defend and represent this man, I made up my mind that I am not going to back down. If I have to try to defend him, I am going to do it to the best of my ability, and the only thing that helps me out is this: that as low as his industry stands below that of bootlegging, yet so high does it stand above these other two birds represented here.

TAKES A FLING AT LANDIS

"Take this man Landis—this little glorified rounder thing that has come here with this thing baseball. What is baseball? Baseball is not an industry, and as the Yankees play it, it is not even a game. It doesn't mean anything. Well, he comes from the bench—he is the only man in the history of the world that ever jumped from the bench into the grandstand. Most players go from the bench into the grandstand. I happened to be up there one evening when the sun was shining about three o'clock on a certain afternoon over Coogan's Bluff, and the game was called on account of darkness, and I thought at that time when those ten thousand people were howling around his box that his next jump would be from the box to the scaffold.

"I am only trying to prove my case with my man, with my little client. Ladies and gentlemen, I am only trying to prove to you that the intelligence of a baseball audience is even lower than the movies. They thought he called the game! Now, what do you think of that? If you can beat that! Well, that shows the degree of intelligence to which his

industry caters. The umpire called the game--
naturally. Now, I will say this for the baseball fan.
A baseball fan is not supposed to know much—but
he does know night from day. And if this man did
not know enough to appoint an umpire that knows
light from dark, how is the umpire going to tell a
ball from a strike? Now, they caught on to that.
You say that that was about the lowest form of
intelligence that there is, as demonstrated by the
baseball. But it is not.

"Absolutely, they have gathered another industry
here tonight which is even lower than that—even
worse than the others. We have tonight another
one that came in years ago in Rome—and has been
in all of the ancient cities—London, Oklahoma City—
all of the old towns. In these there used to be a
bunch of people who went about the streets making
faces, and the people would throw them bouquets.
Busking, they call it. Busking—they were buffoons,
mountebanks—it didn't mean anything—and somebody conceived the idea of taking these people in off
the street, and putting them in a theater or something, and through charity putting a roof over their
heads. I think that it was Marcus Loew that built
the first one.

"He brought them into the theater. To give you
an idea of the intelligence that is exemplified—represented in one of these temples of art. Well, I
wandered into it one day, and the first thing that
comes out on the stage and greets me, is a rough,
uncouth person with no refinement, no intelligence,
with not even a half regard for the English language.

Well, Gentlemen, evidently this individual had
been raised close to a livery stable, and he comes
out on this stage with a lot of ropes and jumps
back and forth through these ropes like a monkey,
or something.   His remarks were of the same
Simian variety, and chewing about something like
a cow, or a cud.   Now, absolutely, after seeing this,
Gentlemen, you know, a man of my refinement, I
say absolutely that it was repulsive to me and now
that is one of the gentlemen that Mr. Thomas represents in his industry.

"Mr. Landis says 'That is fine,' as he says when
Babe Ruth goes all around the country and plays
baseball, he says, 'I am going to set him down for
forty days.'   But now it comes down to Mr. Hopper
running around here and he should be made to live
with the same wife for forty days.

"And now, tonight, we get these gentlemen together at this big dinner.   When this big dinner of
the Friars was first talked about, they asked, 'Who
is Landis?'   'Well, he was a Judge.'

" 'Where?'

" 'He was a Judge out in Chicago.'

"They said, right away the theatrical people
would say, 'Well, that will never do.   New York
won't stand for a Chicago production.'   But that
was put out because Judge Landis was not known,
that is, here in theatrical circles—he is only known
in baseball and the Standard Oil.

"Then it comes down to Will Hays.   What about
Will Hays?   And somebody says, 'We can't give
a dinner to Will Hays.   Will Hays is a Republican

and he says, 'Even if we got all the four Republicans in New York, the dinner wouldn't pay.'

POKES FUN AT AUGUSTUS THOMAS

"But how about Thomas? He is head of the theater and he is a playwright. 'Well,' they says, 'a lot of the members of the Friars, in fact, all of us has written plays—that is no reason just because Thomas has been unfortunate enough to have some of them produced, that is no reason we should give him a dinner.' So it came down to finally the idea was that we can't get a dinner at ten dollars a plate for these men, but how about making it $3.33⅓ apiece, and having them altogether, and having one?

"So the idea appealed to the spirit of the Friars, and so we have got them here tonight—the biggest thing that has ever been held. We have them here tonight—three in one—you know—the big three in one—and if any of you feel prominent enough tonight and will get two other friends together with you, we will give you a dinner.

"Now, gentlemen, in closing I want to say now—*my man*—I am here to defend him with the best I have got in me, and *my little man* that is sitting there—now, mind you, in stature, while I might say he is a Ford in stature, but in intelligence, mind you, in intellect—he is really a Dodge. Now, before he sold his soul into this sinful screen—well he merged his manhood into the murderous movies—this man was respected in the community. He was a man who was held very high. But now he is in the screen, he is in the movies, which as I would

say is the buttonhole end of the amusement
business.

"Here is a man, now, that used to be Postmaster
General of the United States and he had charge of
all of the letters which passed between each and
every one of us and everyone in the United States
and he would have gotten that appointment, with
this wonderful position much sooner, with the
movies, if they had sent it by telegram—but they
sent the announcement by mail.

"When he got his appointment he said, 'Warren,
what will I do?'

"And Warren says, 'Will, how much is in it?'

"And Will says, '$150,000.'

"And Warren says, 'Go on in, Will, and if you see
anything good let me know and I will come in with
you.'

"The Republicans promised the country prosperity, but up to now Hays is the only one that has
got any of it.

"There were two of these Hays boys, there was
Archbishop and Will.   I learn from my good and
dear friend, Father Duffy, that Archbishop Hayes is
soon to be made a Cardinal.   Well, Will had one
hundred and fifty—I tell you these Hays boys are
doing great.

"He absolutely was responsible more than any
other man in the United States for electing Warren
G. Harding, President.   Will Hays took an unknown
man from a front porch at Marion to the stage door
of the White House and he started him in there.
He is the friend and confidential adviser of two

Presidents of the United States, and one was the greatest one which ever we have heard of—Theodore Roosevelt, and one Mr. Harding.

"I know these things to be a fact, because the most cherished thing in my life was meeting these two gentlemen, Mr. Roosevelt and Mr. Harding, and Will Hays was the one who took me in and introduced me to both of them and the reason I know he is great is that he didn't knock either of them—and he didn't knock at the door—he just went on in.

"Now, I want to say that my little man, he is the confidential friend, personal adviser, and right-hand man of not only two Presidents, but he was feared and respected by another for eight years, and in the words of our illustrious Abbot, George M. Cohan, all I can say about him is that he is a great little guy."

ROGERS "TAKES UP" AL SMITH

Willie Collier was toastmaster the night the Friars gave a dinner to their fellow member Al Smith, Governor of New York State and later Democratic nominee for President.

Collier introduced Rogers as follows: "I present my old friend and fellow actor with the toughest spot on the bill."

"This guy must be a great bird," said Will Rogers. "If he is not a great bird, we have the greatest conglomeration of liars ever gathered together on the Lord's earth.

"Some of it that we heard were lies, the chances are a great deal of it were lies, because no man could live and be that good and great—not in New York.

he couldn't, and not in politics. So, I am one of the speakers that will not sell my pride and stand up here and lie for a mere dinner. They are better educated than I am—the speakers who have preceded me—but they haven't got any more honor than I have so I will not sell myself for a mere meal.

"As I say—I want to take up Mr. Smith—I am glad that none of them discovered him under the shade of the Brooklyn Bridge. I want to find him there. It seems that they didn't discover him until after he had a change of shirts when he got up in political life. I found him when South Street and Oliver Street was North America to him, and if a man ever left that neighborhood and go as far north as Fourteenth Street, he was a globe trotter.

"He was born under the shadow of Brooklyn Bridge. He saw Brooklyn Bridge in his youth, he saw them build Brooklyn Bridge—and Brooklyn Bridge is the greatest ad that Brooklyn ever had. If some man had accidentally named that bridge 'New York Bridge' there never would have been any Brooklyn.

"As a youth he grew up there—the nearest place was the fire house, fire engine company No. 32. John Binns, Captain—am I right? Yes, sir! He grew up there. The first ten years of his life he spent—in those days they used horses with fire engines—the first ten years of his life, he spent chasing after the fire wagon running to fires. He got so adept at this that he could tell by the smell of the smoke whose house was burning.

"At the age of eleven, somebody invented a fireproof house, and he lost his job. At twelve he learned elocution. He learned elocution and also learned to dive off the docks in the East River; the last accomplishment was far more beneficial. Through running to these fires is where he got the running experience for some twenty political races. He is the only 'man in public life that never will run for an office—he never gave up the one he was holding to run for another one. He always held one. When he was running for the presidential nomination, he was still Governor; he always had the ace in the hole. There were no open weeks in his career.

"At the age of thirteen, his father died, and left him the sole support of his mother and sister. His father was a truckman, had his team of horses and worked very hard, and left this young boy to support the family. Now Al could have taken up the trucking business in those days but the horses would not listen to the elocution.

"So he got a job in the Fulton Fish Market. Fish are not very discriminating in what is said in their presence. Fish are the only things in the world perhaps that will listen to you recite. He worked there for years. He worked in this fish market there for seven years. At the end of four years—he worked there seven years, but at the end of four years, as the recitations grew longer the live fish had him transferred to the dead fish department. Working in this fish market led him into his political career and he has been talking to 'fish' ever since.

"Last summer in Madison Square Garden was gathered I suppose the greatest collection of fish in the annals of this country.   In that collection last summer in Madison Square Garden, at that gathering there were 'suckers' from the South, there were 'bloaters' from the West, there were 'bullheads' from the North, and there were 'eels' from the East.

"To show you it was a 'fish' collection, they had to hold the convention in a swimming pool and every one of them that got up to make a speech was a big-mouthed bass.

"At the age of eighteen, Al was given a silver medal for debating.   That is the only year's work he ever lost.   The next year he was polishing this medal.   During the time he tried to keep this medal from tarnishing, he took to amateur theatricals, which is the lowest brand of theatricals in the world.   It is bad enough to be a 'ham,' but when you are a 'ham' for nothing, it is terrible.

AL SMITH'S COURTSHIP

"He fell in love with a girl, Catherine Dunn, and odd to say, he is still in love with her.   He fell in love with a girl whose family was—was Irish. People in those days fell in love with ones of their own nationality.   When the Dunns heard that Al, the actor-for-nothing, was snooping around, they moved to the Bronx, thinking they would be done with Al, but they didn't know our Al.   By the way, when the Dunns moved to the Bronx, they were the first and the last Irish family that ever went there. Al heard about the Bronx and, on account of training for a theatrical career, he walked up there. When he got to the Bronx, they had to give him the girl to get rid of him. He stayed around there and they practically sacrificed Catherine to keep from feeding Al.

"But, before giving the girl over in marriage to Al, they disapproved of this acting business. So he had them come and see him in one of his plays, 'The Shogun.' They came to see Al play, and after they saw him acting they withdrew their objections on that account. They said, 'Daughter, we were wrong. Your sweetheart is not an actor.' The Dunns at that time thought that acting was about the lowest profession that there was, naturally. They had never thought of a politician.

"He took his young bride back down where they were raised, down on—well, they got high-toned and moved to Oliver Street. That was the Palm Beach of its time. They moved to Oliver Street and Al Smith has always lived down there with these people—in the first days it was all Irish. It was all Irish that lived in this neighborhood. The Jews came along and raised the rent and the Irish had to get out. The Jews only stayed there two or three years, and they made enough to emi-- grate North. In the early days our forefathers went across the plains in a covered wagon, but due to Mayor Hylan and the five-cent fare, they emigrated to the Bronx for a nickel. Then in come the Wops, in this very district. The Wops stayed in there a while. and along come the Greeks and run them out, so now he is living down there among the Greeks in his same old neighborhood, because he figures that a Greek vote is just as much as an Irish vote. It doesn't make any difference whose vote it is. They go to the polls and vote for Al Smith. They vote for him for anything—they put down Al Smith for everything from President down to Alderman or whatever it might be—they know he's running for something, and they're going to get him. You have a great collection of people here in this hall tonight, all the Irish and Jewish people. The Irish are here to lord it over the other fellows—the Irish nationality you know—they are here to boast that Al is one of them. The Jews are here, you know, to stand in with him so he'll cut the income tax down. So, they had to send out and get a lone Protestant to come in, the only Protestant in the Hall who had nerve to tell the truth about it.

"Now, I want to tell you what the people of New York think of Al Smith. As I spoke of a while ago— during this epidemic of Democratic hydrophobia which prevailed in Madison Square Garden last summer, or through the biggest part of last year, it was my misfortune to have to report that affair. I used to have to go down there every day from the hotel—I live right here in this hotel—I had to rush down there to cover that convention.

"And on account of this old homely mug and because of my working in pictures and a little of everything trying to make a living, I am known by most of the taxi drivers and cops in this town. None of the good people know me, but all of these fellows know me by sight. When I would come

out of that convention hall and start up to the
theater to work a matinee, at the last minute, I
would have the big cop—he would not have to be
Irish or any other nationality, but he would rush up
to me, 'How was the last vote?' There would be a
tremor in his voice when he would ask me 'How
is the last vote? Are they still giving him the
vote?' And I would say, 'Yes.' 'Has he got a
chance?' I says, 'Well, I think he has, he is going
all right, fine.' And I would get into a taxicab,
the driver was the toughest mug in the world, whom
you would not think knew whether our President
was elected or the job was hereditary, and before
he would start, he would turn to me and say, 'How is
Al doing, are they going to beat him, how is he doing?'

POPULARITY OF AL SMITH

"Everywhere you would go—when I would come
into the theater, the minute I would rush in the
stage door every stage hand would rush up and say,
'How is the vote, is Al gaining, do you think? Those
crooks aren't going to beat him, do you think?'
Every one of them. The manager of the theater
would come back and want to know how everything
was. He would say, 'You were down there, you
talked to those delegates, how is he going?' And
I would say, 'Well, I think everything is all right,
it looks like he is holding his own fine.'

"I have seen news kids on the street, where the
headlines came out that he had lost in the vote,
absolutely with no heart to sell their papers, if he
was not ahead.

"That is the man I am speaking about right here tonight. Those are just the things I have seen in those times. I have come into this hotel and the elevator boys would ask me before they would start the elevator, 'How is the vote, what do you think, ain't they going to nominate him? Gee, everybody wants him.' I would go down to the barber shop where every nationality is employed, and the same thing prevailed. I talked with the delegates from all over the West and everywhere and they said, 'What manner of man is this man Smith, that everybody is so crazy about him, what sort of a fellow is this?' I said, 'I don't know, you have got to meet him, that is all, to really know him, and these people meet him and they do know him.

"I'll bet you that during that convention you could have called for a draft of men to give up their lives for this nomination, and you would have found as many would have done it as will go to the next war. That is what they thought of him.

"Now, you can't get that kind of admiration on nothing. You have to do something to have people as cuckoo as that about you, especially if you have gone twenty-three years. He has twenty-three years of public service. Now, you cannot get it. You must have done something in all that time. Because while he might fool us Christians that long, you Jews would have got wise in two years.

"Let me tell you something. This goes with all of the Tammany Hall organization here, and all: 'Al Smith don't owe New York one thing. Al Smith don't owe Tammany Hall one thing. Tammany

Hall, as far as national officers are concerned, is a detriment, and was a detriment to Al Smith. You know as well as I do that outside of Tammany Hall, whether it is unearned or not, but outside of that, you know that the people are a little leary of Tammany Hall, and that is not kidding you either. They are leary of you birds, outside of New York. New York was not of any advantage to him, because the people in the other state say, 'Ah! New York, we will give them nothing.' So he had to fight in the face of all of that, and so Al Smith has done more for Tammany Hall than Tammany Hall has ever done for Al Smith. He is the first big public official you ever had here. Since that convention came off, and with all the friends he made through it, he is the first man in public life from Tammany Hall that the rest of the United States today will trust.

"That is not Tammany Hall's fault. It is not New York or anything. You tried to do the best you could for him. That is because they know him better. They know him now. They know he is honest. They know he is square. And no matter —I do not care—you can talk to a Republican, he might not be for him, he might be a rabid Republican—and if you are a Republican, you are rabid— but if you talk about him, everyone will admit that Smith is on the level, I do not care whether he is for him politically or not, he will admit that Smith is on the level, he is a square guy."

CHAPTER XII

Prime Minister of Aviation

WILL ROGERS was the "No. 1 air passenger of the United States," according to the records of two great transcontinental air lines. Aviation experts held it ironical that he should make his final flight while on one of his very rare trips in a privately owned plane and far off the established air lanes with their many safeguards. Rogers preferred travel by air, whether on long or short flights, at home or abroad, and he always preached the doctrine of the safety of flight behind transport pilots in modern planes beating their way over carefully charted paths. He made more than twenty-five crossings of the United States by airplane. That with his other flying made more than 500,000 air miles that he had flown over the country.

Flying meant more to Will Rogers than his lucrative stardom in the movies. It was related that he waived aside a cool million dollars to indulge in his desire to travel by air. It was in regard to a life-insurance policy which carried a double indemnity clause in case of death by violence or accident. The company refused the policy because of Rogers' passion for flying. Rather than agree to stop flying, Rogers had the provision stricken from the policy.

By special permit from Washington, Rogers held a pass that entitled him to travel in airmail planes virtually wherever and whenever he chose, regardless of whether they carried passengers regularly. It is said he was the first unofficial person ever to hold such a permit.

A STAUNCH SUPPORTER OF AVIATION

What the permit meant to him was shown by the fact that he carefully preserved every passage receipt for all his air trips and kept an itemized account of all expenses involved in his flights. Will had preached the doctrine of air travel so consistently that he had an idea he might some day be accused of being a paid propagandist for the air lines. He was anxious to avoid such a charge and he would not accept a free ride from an air-line company although it would have been given gladly. He frequently used the radio in behalf of aviation. On one occasion before going on the radio he said:

"Wait till you hear the boost I have tonight for traveling in airplanes! I bet a lot of guys will be on my neck tomorrow, saying some airplane company paid me a lot of money to knock the railroads."

On another occasion he wired his daily comment to the McNaught Syndicate from El Paso, Texas, with high praise for the safety of flight. That was in April, 1931, as he was about to start his Central American tour. It was shortly after Knute Rockne, famed Notre Dame football coach, was killed in an airplane crash. It read:

"Had a great trip in here today over the American Airways passenger line. Kelsey, the pilot, has flown 400,000 miles without a sign of a mishap.

"Glad to hear in Los Angeles this morning from the different air lines that the late accident [the crack-up in which Rockne was killed] did not interfere with travel.

"Why, my hair turned from gray to white just fifteen minutes ago, in a taxi going over to Juarez, when a Mexican missed us by inches. Would have given my life to have been in a plane."

On one occasion he was to ride an airmail plane between Los Angeles and New York. For the fun of the thing, Rogers appeared at the airport attired in a swanky aviator's costume of soft, brown leather.

"I'm just going to New York to have dinner with a couple of fellers," he said, as he laughed at his attire.

The pilot entered into the spirit of the occasion and insisted that since Rogers had on new flying gear he must be without much flying experience. He told Rogers they would have to have a rehearsal on the use of the parachute and ordered him to jump from the cockpit of the plane and count ten before pulling the ripcord.

"If I have to use that thing," said Rogers, patting his parachute, "ten 'll be an awful short count. They gave Gene Tunney a count of fourteen."

AIRMEN, FAVORITES OF ROGERS

Rogers was a friend of all the famous fliers of his time. He had flown several times with Colonel Charles A. Lindbergh and was an intimate friend of the Lone Eagle. Rogers was one of the few persons that had visited the Colonel and Anne Morrow

Lindbergh in their secluded home on Sourland Mountain. There Will had played with the Lindbergh's firstborn, Charles A. Lindbergh, Jr., the baby who was kidnaped and murdered.

Frank Hawks, noted speed king of the air, was another favorite pilot of Rogers. Hawks, himself from the Southwest, had flown Rogers thousands of miles through that section on charity missions in behalf of drought and unemployment victims in Texas in 1931. As a part of their act, Rogers taught Frank to make a speech. The flier, however, unconsciously picked up many of Will's mannerisms and quaint expressions.

"I sometimes think I'm Will Rogers," Hawks once told a group of actors. As he made the remark, he reached up and scratched his head in the familiar Rogers manner. It created an uproar.

But Wiley Post, with whom he died, was Rogers' favorite. On the occasion of dedicating the landing field at Claremore, Oklahoma, Rogers said:

"It wasn't ambition that drove Wiley Post up in the air. It was the boll weevil. Wiley used to be on a cotton farm. If it hadn't been for the Republican administration, he might have remained an underfed, overmortgaged farmer. So you got to quit knocking the Republicans; they really made Wiley Post what he is.

"He got his mechanical knowledge from working in a garage. He worked in cahoots with a feller in the next town and they got so's they could fix a car so it would fall entirely apart when it reached the other feller's place.

"A plane crashed one day near Wiley's garage and all that was left intact was the propeller. So Wiley took it, put it on a flivver in place of a fan, and flew with it on a solo flight.

"Wiley was raised on a Texas 'norther' and weaned on an Oklahoma cyclone."

Crashes were nothing new in Rogers' experience in the air, two of them happened in one day in 1928. On that day he had taken off from Omaha in a specially chartered plane and was forced down at Cherokee, near Cheyenne, Wyoming. One of the wheels hit a gopher hole and was torn off. Rogers went on to Cheyenne by automobile and boarded a mail plane, which turned over on its back as they were landing at Las Vegas, New Mexico.

"Wheel broke when she come down and turned over and lit on her head," he said. "Am the first candidate to land on his head, but being a candidate it didn't hurt the head."

JOKED ABOUT DEATH IN THE AIR

Time after time, Rogers told friends that some of his best quips were written "in the air." In recent years he never would take a train or a boat if he could go by airplane. He scoffed at the idea of danger.

"Those flying fellows at the controls," he once told David Butler, his director, "have as much to lose as me. They're young fellows, most of 'em and they have their whole lives ahead of them. Old Will has had his fun and enjoyed every minute of it."

On another occasion he carried his humor into a conversation about death in the air. Senator Pat Harrison, of Mississippi, told Rogers "he ought to cut out flying; that he was going to be killed."

"But he merely told me," Harrison related, "that I would be killed trying to hit a golf ball."

Rogers was in New York when Roosevelt canceled the airmail contracts. The studio at Hollywood needed him at once and telephoned, but he replied that he could not come as passenger-plane schedules had been abandoned. The film company officials told him to come by train, but he refused.

Finally he procured a plane and went as far as Texas, when adverse weather interrupted the flight. Will telephoned the studio that "he was getting close." Again the movie people tried to get him to take a train but he waited until the plane was able to get through.

AN INVETERATE AIR TRAVELER

In December, 1927, Will was on one of his periodical trips to Mexico. He was one of the 50,000 spectators that waited seven hours at the Mexico City airport for Colonel Charles A. Lindbergh to end his nonstop flight from Washington. He sat in the principal stand with President Calles and Ambassador Morrow, who later became Lindbergh's father-in-law, while the Lone Eagle of the Atlantic was fighting his way through fog to reach his destination. On that visit to Mexico, he was taken aloft by Lindbergh for a flight over the Mexican mountains in *The Spirit of St. Louis*.

Rogers made his first flight in 1925 and he flew under all sorts of weather conditions. He once rode in a Navy plane when it was catapulted along a sixty-foot runway into the air. Needless to say, Rogers enjoyed the thrilling experience immensely. In 1926 while visiting Europe, he traveled by air from Rome to Paris and twice from London to Berlin. From the German capital he flew on to Moscow.

Among Rogers' ambitions was the desire to become the "world's airplane reporter." He wanted to have his own plane fitted up and spend his time flying around the world to the points where the big news of the day was happening and record his observations. His flight to the Manchurian battlefields, to Mexico, South America, and around Europe were all in line with his idea of being an aërial newspaper man. He never learned to fly a plane himself, it was said, because he had promised Mrs. Rogers he would not. His wife, however, became an enthusiastic air traveler herself.

Rogers always placed confidence in the pilots and he delighted in becoming personally acquainted with them. He never tired of talking with flying men, and of them he remarked:

"This thing about somebody's life being too valuable to risk in an airplane is the bunk. It's an insult to the men we ask to do our flying."

On one trip from New York to the coast, Rudy Vallee, the radio star, was a passenger on the plane. Commenting on it in his daily news feature, he wrote:

14

"I've made this trip by air 100 times but I never saw such mobs at the fields. Rudy Vallee is on our ship. I am just as excited as they are, and say, he is a very modest, likable young fellow. I was even flattered when the folks at Amarillo thought I was his father."

"DEAN" OF THE FRIARS

Rogers thought nothing of hopping into an airplane in California and "high-tailing it" to New York. On one occasion, the Friars Club wanted to honor him by making him dean of the club. Friar Vic Guinness, artist and illustrator, drew a striking likeness of Rogers as a tribute to him. More than 500 members of the club put their autographs on the picture and it was sent to him without a word of explanation.

Charles Pope, secretary of the Friars, later called him up on the long-distance telephone and said: "Bill, that is what we think of you. The boys who autographed that picture want you to be dean of the club."

Rogers stammered: "Why, uh, it's a grand picture. Vic did a swell job. Wait—I'll be in New York tomorrow."

He then rushed out and boarded a plane at Los Angeles. The next day, according to his promise, he walked into the Friars Club.

"I appreciate the honor," Rogers explained to Pope, "but I can't take it. I'm not in New York much any more and anyway, George Jessel makes a swell dean. He ought to be reëlected."

Will then hurried from the club, boarded another transcontinental plane and was homeward bound after only a little more than an hour in New York.

His electioneering for Jessel was successful and George was reëlected.

Major General John F. O'Ryan, of New York, recalled meeting Rogers and Frank Hawks at Fort Worth while they were making their relief flights. O'Ryan told Rogers that Hawks' plane was exceptionally fast and the pair might just as well be riding a comet.

"Yep," answered Rogers, "but we are specialists with comets."

The fact that Franklin D. Roosevelt flew out to Chicago to accept the nomination for President pleased Rogers immensely.

"Looks like we're going to have a President with nerve enough to fly," he declared.

One of the last articles Rogers wrote for his Sunday syndicate feature showed the great love that he had for the air. He said that his feet were bad and his legs worse, "so I take mine out in riding in the air."

He told how they flew over Mount Shasta, coming very close to the summit. He described the beautiful mountain as "snow all over the old ant hill." Commenting upon their stop at Medford, Oregon, he took occasion to poke a little fun at an "ambitious reporter" from that city who "had sent out a dispatch that he had seen Wiley Post and me flying over there, when we were at that time crossing Arizona."

"This time," Will wrote, "he is liable to report that I arrived there by horse and buggy."

He recalled that in his vaudeville days in 1908 he played in Tacoma and that was the first city that had a slogan. It read: "Watch Tacoma Grow."

"I never watched it much since," commented Will, "but it did.

"A plane is a great place to see anything, only the wings are right under where you want to look and you can't see anything. I really did see Mount Shasta. They couldn't hide that under the wings."

CHAPTER XIII

FLYING WITH WILEY POST

THE PLANS of Will Rogers and Wiley Post were vague when they took-off from Seattle early in August for "the roof of the world"—Point Barrow—the northernmost outpost of civilization on the North American continent. It was to be a vacation trip by easy stages with no particular destination. Rogers was paying the expenses of the jaunt and they had half-formed plans of flying around the world by way of Siberia, China, Ethiopia, Europe, and Greenland. Their plane was a hybrid Lockheed with a new Wasp 550-horse-power engine, the wings of a cracked-up Sirius, and the fuselage of a wrecked Orion. It was equipped with pontoons for landing on water. Some experts said that the added floats made the ship too heavy, but Post was too good a flier to take his best friend in a flying job that was not entirely airworthy.

From Seattle the vacationists hopped to Juneau, Alaska, where Rogers met his old friend, Rex Beach; then they went on to Dawson, Aklavik, Fairbanks, Anchorage, and the Government's great experiment in pioneering, the Matanuska Valley. At Matanuska, the colonists swarmed around the plane as Rogers was climbing out.

"How do you feel, Mr. Rogers?" someone shouted.

"Why, uh, why—wait'll I get out, will you?" wisecracked Will. "I came to look around, not report on my health."

"Where you boys from?" he asked as the crowd jostled one another to get a closer look at him. "Anybody here from Claremore?"

The colonists doubled up with laughter as Will stood in weeds that reached up to the knees of his corduroy breeches and joked. Rogers spent about ninety minutes looking over the valley.

GREETS MATANUSKA PIONEERS

"The valley looks great," he told the pioneers. "It looks fine, fine. You got a mighty nice place here. We saw some colonists. Caught one guy just moving his stove in. I said, 'I'd just as soon be moving in with him.'"

"How do you think you'll like Russia?" asked one of the crowd.

"Russia? Russia?" replied Will, feigning ignorance of the fact it was generally known he planned to fly there. "I saw a communist here a minute ago. There he is now."

He pointed to a construction worker with a full, red beard that reached down to the middle of his blue work shirt. The worker and the crowd joined in the roar that followed. A cook from the transient workers' camp came up and presented Will with six brown, thick cookies.

"They're great," said Rogers, brushing the crumbs from his lips with the sleeve of his coat. "But I'll toss 'em out if we can't get the plane off the ground."

That crowd of hardy pioneers in the wilds of Alaska was Will Rogers' last audience. Showman Rogers—he left them roaring with laughter.

Post stood almost forgotten while Rogers played his final "stand," but as far as the humorist was concerned, the bushy-haired flier from Oklahoma was the greatest of flying men and he paid tribute to him whenever the opportunity afforded. Above all, Rogers admired the grit and determination that had won Post his wings among the ace fliers of the world.

Rogers and Post, both flying enthusiasts, met while the flier was being fêted for his around-the-world trip, which he accomplished in 1931 in eight days, fifteen hours, fifty-one minutes. The comedian flew with Post at that time, and from then on the two were the closest of friends. The two were direct opposites. Rogers was voluble; Post always taciturn. One thing they both had in common was the love of speed. Post piloted a plane as Rogers rode horses—full speed ahead. The Oklahoma flier was one of the few pilots that was equal to the strain of flying hour after hour with a "full gun"; that is, with the engine going always at its maximum speed. Post, however, liked his speed in air. On the ground he was content with thirty miles an hour in an automobile.

THEIR LAST TAKE-OFF

After the flight to the Matanuska project, which was made in a Lockheed plane placed at their disposal by Joe Crosson, chief pilot of the Pacific

Alaska Airways, they returned to Fairbanks on August 14. The following day they took-off on the tragic flight to the north. Before they left, Rogers sat down at his portable typewriter and sent the following news despatch to the more than 350 newspapers that used his feature daily:

"Fairbanks, Alaska, Aug. 15.—Visited our new emigrants. Now, this is no time to discuss whether it will succeed or whether it won't; whether it's farming country or whether it is not, and to enumerate the hundreds of mistakes and confusions and rows and arguments and management in the whole thing at home and here.

"As I see it, there is now but one problem now that they are here, and that's to get 'em housed within six or eight weeks. Things have been a terrible mess. They are getting 'em straightened out, but even now not fast enough. There is about 700 or 800 of 'em. About 200 went back; also about that many workmen sent from the transient camps down home (not CCC) and just lately they are using about 150 Alaskan workmen at regular wages. But it's just a few weeks to snow now and they have to be out of the tents, both workmen and settlers.

"There is plenty food and always has been and will be. They can always get that in, but it's houses they need right now and Colonel Hunt, in charge, realizes it.

"You know, after all, there is a lot of difference in pioneering for gold and pioneering for spinach.

"Yours, WILL ROGERS"

It was not until the next day, however, that the world heard how the two ended that flight in the Alaskan barrens, only a few miles from their destination. It is not too much to say that the whole world grieved at the passing of Rogers. Certainly, no private citizen ever before was accorded so many millions of words of eulogy in the newspapers as were written about Rogers. No one man ever before was the subject of so much comment in the everyday conversation of the people.

WILEY POST, AN INSPIRATION

Post was a younger man, whose accomplishment was in the theater of action. He had not captivated the hearts of the millions as had Rogers, but in the nearly thirty-six years that he lived, he achieved more than most men do in the reputed full life of "threescore years and ten." Post died flying, and that was a "happy landing," according to his scheme of things. He left behind a flying log that all of his contemporaries could envy. His biography stands as an inspiration to the youth of America.

From the obscurity of the Southwestern plains Post lifted himself to the heights of world fame after surmounting difficulties that would have overwhelmed a lesser character. He became one of the greatest aërial pioneers in the history of aëronautics, and his adventures in the substratosphere cast him in the rôle of a character from a Jules Verne fantasy. Those flights of his into the unknown regions that lie only about ten miles directly above everyone's head provided highly important scien-

tific information that was seized upon by aëronau-
tical engineers as the basis of designs for future
aircraft.

He won acclaim—but little money—and through
it all he remained the most modest of pilots. Post's
exploits were varied.   There was his record of
twenty-five hours and forty-five minutes from New
York to Berlin in 1933, one of the greatest and
most accurate flights of aërial navigation ever made
up to that time.   As a cross-country flier, he was
without a peer.

BECOMES TRANSPORT PILOT

While a young man in the Texas oil fields, he lost
the sight of one eye; but despite his disfigurement,
he carried on through the early stages of training as
a flier and after many objections convinced Government officials that he was entitled to a rating as a
transport pilot.   Because of his handicap, he was
compelled to fly many more hours—actually seven
times as many—than is customary for other pilots.
He financed his early training as a pilot by working
in the oil fields.

Post first came into prominence as a pilot in
1930 when, to the astonishment of more seasoned
fliers, he showed them the way from Los Angeles
into Chicago to win the Derby of the National Air
Races.   His plane, the *Winnie Mae*, was owned by
F. C. Hall, an Oklahoman oil man.   In it Post
made most of his subsequent records.   The trim
white-and-blue monoplane, which was purchased by
the Government to be placed in the Smithsonian

Institution alongside Lindbergh's famous plane, *The Spirit of St. Louis*, was Post's greatest joy.

Wiley Post was born in Grand Saline, Texas, November 22, 1899, and like Rogers, there was a trace of Indian blood in his veins, a heritage of several generations of Southwestern pioneers. His great-grandfather was a Baptist preacher and his parents, descendants of Scotch-Irish stock, wrested a living from the soil. Wiley was the fourth of six children, and from his boyhood he was interested in the machinery used on the Post farm. Early in his youth he determined to become a flier; but he was an indifferent student, being more interested in drawing models of airplanes than in learning the rudiments of grammar. Outside of the mechanical end of farming, he had no interest in agriculture. His fine mechanical sense, however, made him the neighborhood handy man. Post saw his first airplane in 1913 when he visited the county fair at Lawton, Oklahoma, while his parents were living in Chickasha. It was an old Curtiss "pusher," flown by Art Smith, then one of the veteran birdmen. During the World War, Wiley enlisted in the Signal Corps and hoped he would get a chance to fly, but the War Department took aviation out of the corps and made it a separate branch. After the war, Post went to work in an automobile-repair shop and a few months later signed on as a "roughneck" in the oil fields.

He said of that part of his career:

"We got seven dollars a day, but the work was hard and dirty. Sometimes I fed boilers; sometimes I had to climb the derrick to thread pulleys, and at other times I drove cars. The gambling fever of the oil fields hit me hard. My first stake went into a wildcat scheme, but I went back to work as a driller and made another stake at twenty-five dollars a day."

PARACHUTE JUMPER

It was in the summer of 1919 that Post took his first ride in an airplane. He paid twenty-five dollars for the ride and was flown by a man he never further identified than as "Captain Zimmerman." Four and a half years later he embarked on the aviation career which terminated in the Arctic.

At Wewoka, Oklahoma, a flying circus was stationed, and after much persuasion, Post obtained one assignment as a parachute jumper. Berl Tibbs, an old barnstormer, was the pilot. His first parachute landing nearly ended in disaster. With some practice, however, Post became proficient at jumping and put in two years, during which he took his first dual instruction from one of the pilots, Sam Bartel.

It was 1926 before he made his first solo flight, of which he said:

"It wasn't until I had wobbled down the rough ground and cleared the fence that I realized I was alone in the plane. For the first time in my life I was almost frightened. I climbed to where I felt comfortable and flew around until I was sufficiently sure of myself to attempt a landing. I forgot to clear the motor out and nearly ended in a forced

landing.   I discovered later that I barely missed a
tree with the right wing before I pulled the ship up
again and slipped in over the fence a bit high.   I
got the thing down without breaking anything and
called it a day."

Lack of business in aviation sent the flier back to
the oil fields in December, 1925.   His first day on
the field lost him his eye and apparently blasted his
hopes of becoming an airplane pilot.   A "roughneck," driving an iron bolt through the derrick,
chipped a piece from his sledge which flew into
Post's left eyeball.   The eye had to be removed
when an infection set in.

POST GETS HIS TICKET

Post related recently how he took the $1,800
compensation for his eye, practiced depth perception
with his other eye until his sight was superior to
that of his two eyes, and bought his first airplane.
In it on June 27, 1927, he eloped from Sweetwater,
Texas, with Miss Mae Laine.   In the getaway in the
airplane, he had a forced landing in a cornfield.

Next year he took a place as personal pilot to
F. C. Hall.   The first ship he flew was a Travelair
open-cockpit machine, which he used for a year.
Then his employer bought a cabin plane and he
spent another year in that.

With the cabin plane his employer insisted that
Post conform to the regulations of the Department
of Commerce and take out a license.   He could not
pass the eye examinations, of course, and it was only
after he had piled up 700 hours of flying the machine

that the Government officials finally granted him his ticket.   He completed the 700 hours in eight months.

Depression then set into the oil industry, and Post obtained a place with the Lockheed Aircraft Corporation as a test pilot.   He went on demonstration tours, competed in the 1929 National Reliability Tour for the Edsel Ford Trophy, and did experimental work, which later stood him in good stead in his own record-making flights.   He also spent some time flying between El Paso and Brownsville, Texas, and Mazatlan, Mexico.

In 1930 his former employer decided to buy another plane, and Post was assigned to supervise its construction.   That plane was the now famous *Winnie Mae*, which carried him to all of his records. In it he won the classic of the 1930 National Air Races at Chicago and came into national prominence as a pilot.

AROUND THE WORLD WITH GATTY

On June 23, 1931, he and Harold Gatty, a navigator, took off from Roosevelt Field, Long Island, and started around the world.

With stops at Harbor Grace, Newfoundland; Chester, England; Berlin, Moscow, Novo-Sibirsk, Irkutsk, Blagoveshchensk and Khabarovsk, Siberia, Solomon Beach in Alaska, Edmonton in Alberta, and Cleveland, they arrived back at Roosevelt Field in exactly eight days, fifteen hours, and fifty-one minutes in the most dramatic flight in history up to that time.

Gatty became navigation instructor to the Army Air Corps as a result of that flight. Post resumed his duties as a pilot after purchasing the *Winnie Mae* from his employer. He held an agency for airplane distribution in the Southwest and then began new experiments.

He equipped his plane with a robot pilot and in July, 1933, repeated his flight around the world. It was in the course of that flight that he established the record to Berlin. His record around the world he lowered to seven days, eighteen hours, and forty-nine minutes.

In 1934 he designed and appeared in his familiar "Man from Mars" flying suit. It was of rubber and capable of inflation to make possible constant pressures at high altitudes. He had his airplane engine specially supercharged and began a series of assaults on the altitude records. In one of his flights he claimed an altitude of more than 49,000 feet but trouble with the barograph prevented his record from becoming official.

His altitude experiments were merely incidental to his real purpose in exploring the substratosphere as a medium to high-speed transport, however, and he abandoned them in favor of cross-country flights at high levels.

Four times he was thwarted by mechanical failures in trying to lower the transcontinental record. Each time he took off from Los Angeles and dropped the landing gear of his plane to lessen the wind resistance. Once he was forced down on a dried lake in the Mojave Desert, another time he came down in Lafayette, Indiana; a third time in Cleveland, and the last time at Wichita, Kansas, on June 15, 1935. His plane, *Winnie Mae*, was about worn out and ready to retire.

Returning to California, he ordered the plane in which he so suddenly met death. He planned a vacation in a leisurely jaunt backward over his route from Moscow. He planned to stop off in Alaska, fly out over Kamchatka to Siberia, and revisit some of the people who had aided him on his two former globe-circling flights.

Post received the Distinguished Flying Cross in 1932 by Act of Congress, received the Collier Trophy for the outstanding feat in aviation that year, won the Gold Medal of Belgium and a $700 prize founded by the late King Albert in 1934, and the Harmon Trophy of the Federation Aëronautique Internationale, of Paris, the same year. He also held the F. A. I. International Gold Medal.

CROSSON'S SAD JOURNEY HOME

The sad duty of bringing back the bodies of Will Rogers and Wiley Post to civilization fell upon Joe Crosson, noted pilot of the Arctic and the one flier best qualified for the task. Post and Crosson were good friends. They met when Crosson flew to aid Post on his solo, globe-girdling flight after the latter had damaged a propeller. At that time, Crosson brought Post a new propeller and the around-the-world flier was able to go on and set a record. Before the northward flight, Post recalled Crosson's help and said, "Oh, Joe will help us out."

But neither Rogers nor Post had any premonition of danger. In fact, Rogers smiled at the thought, in an interview in Portland, Oregon, a few days before the tragedy.

"When are you going to write a book on your life?" interviewers asked Will.

"I don't know," he replied. "I ain't near enough dead yet. One publisher has been after me a long time to write my memoirs. But shucks, you got to be old and pretty near dead to have anything to look back on. I'm a long ways from being dead. Feel just as frisky as a colt."

With the bodies of the two famous Americans strapped to cots, Crosson flew from Point Barrow to Fairbanks, and with scarcely any rest, continued down the coast to Seattle. There he turned the job over to W. A. Winston, a Pan-American Lines pilot, who flew to Los Angeles where Rogers' body was taken out. Then he flew on to Oklahoma City where the funeral services were to be held for Post.

It was the longest funeral journey ever undertaken in the air. Crosson did not stop at Los Angeles, where vast throngs were waiting to pay homage to Rogers. He remained with his brother flier. In the tragic story of that last flight, Crosson is of more than passing interest.

A war-time flier of the top flight, he moved from the easy flying conditions in California in 1926 to face the rigors of aërial exploration in the land of the midnight sun. As a matter of routine, he flew out of Fairbanks on many missions with only his compass and his unerring birdman instinct to guide him over

the trackless wastes.   His exploits won him the
title of "Alaska's mercy flier."

Most famous of his mercy flights were two
hazardous trips to Point Barrow in the dead of an
Arctic winter when he carried serum to fight an
epidemic of influenza which was threatening to wipe
out the Far North outpost in 1931.   The thermometer
registered twenty degrees below zero then and all
flying in Alaska had stopped.   There were blizzards
and heavy winds.

But when Dr. Henry W. Griest, superintendent
of the little Presbyterian Mission Hospital in Point
Barrow, radioed that the entire settlement had been
exposed to influenza, Crosson answered the plea.

He flew a big Fairchild plane in twice with cargoes
of serum.   It was so cold it took him two hours to
warm up his motors whenever he stopped.   But the
settlement was saved.

His first notable exploit was the finding of the
bodies of Carl Ben Eielson and Earl Borland, Alaska
fliers, who were killed when their plane crashed
near North Cape in the Siberian Arctic in the winter
of 1929.   Flying with Frank Dorbandt, Crosson
found the wrecked plane and the bodies far out on the
Arctic ice.   Eielson and Borland had been removing a
valuable fur cargo from the ice-bound fur ship *Nanuk*.

CROSSON'S AIR EXPLOITS

In 1932 Crosson and Jerry Jones flew in search
of Allen Carpe and Theodore Koven, scientists who
were studying the cosmic ray on the slopes of Mount
McKinley, North America's highest peak.

Crosson and Jones found the pair, without food, at an 11,000-foot elevation. They dropped about 100 pounds of concentrated food and supplies which saved the scientists until they could make their way to a level spot where Crosson could land his plane and rescue them.

Those were only a few of Joe Crosson's better known exploits. Alaskans know of the hundreds of trips he has made to rescue a lone trapper, a prospector caught by the sudden advance of winter, a sick man whom only a quick operation would save. There were hundreds of more prosaic but very essential emergency flights, pieces of machinery for an inland mine; supplies for a fish cannery; food for an outpost; a thousand and one of the little tasks which have made Alaska modern, which have condensed weeks and months of arduous travel into a few hours of flying.

MORGAN KNOWN AS "THE LAW"

The other outstanding figure in the tragedy was the one who found pioneering in Alaska the life he wanted. Sergeant Stanley R. Morgan, who organized and directed the rescue expedition, volunteered for duty at Point Barrow when the United States Army Signal Corps decided to put in a radio station there in 1928. The station is known as "Wamcats," or the Washington-American Military Cable and Telegraph System. It was Morgan who flashed the news of the accident over the radio to the world.

In the face of utter isolation, killing cold, and hardships of which city dwellers can have little conception, Morgan not only raised a family at Point Barrow, but acted as "the law," communications agent, Weather Bureau observer, and in a multitude of other capacities on man's farthest north frontier.

Sergeant Morgan worked with Colonel and Mrs. Charles A. Lindbergh when they visited Point Barrow en route to the Orient and he maintained a radio schedule with Mrs. Lindbergh during the Pacific flight. He has kept the world informed of all the news events north of the Arctic Circle and has played his part in relief and rescue expeditions which have engrossed the attention of mankind.

During the influenza epidemic which proved so deadly in Northern Alaska in 1934, Sergeant Morgan and his wife and family all contracted the disease. He had no relief, and, with a high fever, he kept on the job, carrying on all the routine weather work and communications duties and, in addition, sought relief for his sick neighbors and family. Through his efforts, a doctor and nurse finally came through by airplane and dogsled.

Sergeant Morgan designed and largely built his home at Point Barrow. It stands, as do all houses north of the Arctic Circle, on eternal ice. A cellar is carved out of ice under the house and, in that cellar the temperature never rises above ten degrees above zero, although during the summer the daily temperature of the air may range from twenty-nine to thirty-six degrees or so.

The Morgans' home boasts the only porcelain bathtub north of the Arctic Circle, and the tub is

Will Rogers and Wiley Post, just before the vacation flight, in which the noted humorist and the famous flier lost their lives.

Wiley Post, standing in the cockpit, and Will Rogers, as they prepared to take off from Fairbanks, Alaska, on their tragic hop to Point Barrow.

This photograph, taken by Dr. Henry Greist, gives an excellent idea of the desolateness of the country in which Will Rogers and Wiley Post crashed.

famous even as far away as Seattle.   The plumbing line is drawn at Fairbanks.   North of that point, ordinary plumbing is unknown except for the "modernizations" Morgan introduced.

No money is in circulation where Sergeant and Mrs. Morgan hold forth.   All transactions are by primitive barter.   Reindeer meat is the chief food. Geese appear during about thirty days of the year. In order that he may find time to hunt without breaking into the daily radio schedules which must be maintained; Sergeant Morgan has taught his wife to be a relief operator.

The Morgans' elder child, a daughter, was sent back to the United States to school when she was fourteen.   Their other child is a son, named Barrow.

Sergeant Morgan built a snowmobile by putting caterpillar drive and skis on an old flivver and has made trips as long as 200 miles in this vehicle, exploring along the almost unknown coast toward Demarcation Bay.

The thirty-four-year-old Sergeant is the United States Government to the few white men and the few hundred Eskimos north of seventy-one.   He was born in Payson, Utah, in 1901 and enlisted in the Army in 1920.

THE "SPARE-PARTS" PLANE

There was considerable comment over the fact that the plane in which Rogers and Post crashed was a "spare-parts" job but when it was finished, Wiley was proud of her and considered an ideal plane for long-range cruising.   Crosson, too, had inspected the plane when Post brought her to Alaska and was convinced it was a "good job."

In many respects it was similar to the Lockheed Sirius in which Colonel and Mrs. Charles A. Lindbergh made their flights to Japan on a route survey for Pan American Airways.

Fitted to use wheels, skis, or pontoons, as the terrain dictated, the plane had fixed rather than retractable landing gear. It was a composite craft assembled after Post's own ideas, with the fuselage of a Lockheed Orion and a Sirius wing.

The fuselage of the low-wing cantilever monoplane was of oval, wooden monocoque construction. The wing was also of wooden construction, fabric covered. Wheels were fitted at Los Angeles when Post and Rogers made a shake-down flight in the plane into Oklahoma before taking off for the North. Pontoons were fitted in Seattle and were in use instead of wheeled gear when the fatal crash occurred.

The plane was powered with a new Pratt & Whitney raidial air-cooled geared Wasp engine which developed 550 horsepower. The propeller was a three-bladed Hamilton Standard of the controllable pitch type. The angles of the blades could be changed by the pilot from the cockpit to suit conditions of take-off or cruising speed or changes of air density at varying altitudes.

This sleek, low-wing craft was in sharp contrast to the six-year-old *Winnie Mae* in which Post twice circled the world to set new records in aviation. The *Winnie Mae*, a high-wing monoplane of the Vega type, enabled Post to demonstrate the sound-

ness of his belief that greatly increased speed could
be obtained by using the thin airs of the substratosphere.

THOUSANDS PAY RESPECT

Funeral services were held simultaneously for
Rogers and Post in Los Angeles and Oklahoma City.
At the same time in motion-picture houses throughout the land and in hundreds of cities memorial
services were held in honor of the two men. It was
estimated that between 100,000 and 150,000 persons
filed past the catafalque on which the casket of
Rogers rested in Forest Lawn Memorial Park.
Unlike other memorial services that were held in
Los Angeles for other great stars, there was no
pushing or fighting. Respect for Rogers was so
overwhelming that the crowd moved along silently.
A blazing hot sun shone in the heavens but it did
not deter the crowd. Women outnumbered the men
in the crowd by three to one. Among them were
mothers with babies in their arms. On the roads
leading to the memorial park automobiles were
jammed for miles, and thousands were unable to
reach the cemetery. That many of these motorists
had driven many miles to pay their final respects
to the beloved humorist, was shown by the fact that
the automobiles carried numerous out-of-state
licenses, principally from the Middle West.

The morning services for Rogers were simple.
The casket lay under a floral shroud of red and
white carnations and blue sunflowers. It was
closed to the gaze of the curious in accordance with

Mrs. Rogers' request. There were few floral tributes from the throng. The first came from a little, old man—garden blooms that he had raised himself. Then came orchids and other floral pieces, but, according to witnesses, the little man's garden flowers seemed more in keeping with the spirit of the man who had gone.

Beside the bier stood a guard of eight fliers from the Army post at March Field. All morning they stood rigidly at attention guarding the flying friend they had loved so well. The guard was changed every half hour. The first mourner was an admirer of Rogers, M. T. Felso, of Long Beach, who had taken up his place outside the cemetery at 1.30 A. M. For more than six hours he waited before the barrier was swung open and he was allowed to lead the long line of humanity up the huge horseshoe aisle that had been roped off to the casket. Among the first from Hollywood was a little waitress, who worked in a restaurant where Rogers sometimes ate. Will noticed her one day and she was given a chance to play a small part in a picture. She went back to her waitress job, but the kindly act that might have proved her big chance was not forgotten by the girl.

The actual funeral ritual followed the services in the cemetery and were held in the Wee Kirk o' the Heather. They began with organ selections that Will had loved, and included "The Old Rugged Cross," "In the Cross of Christ I Glory," "Beautiful Isle of Somewhere," "Saved by Grace," "I Love to Tell the Story."

John Boles, film star and a close friend of the Rogers family, sang "Old Faithful," and Dr. J. Whitcomb Brougher, associate pastor of the Glendale Baptist Church read the funeral service.

Doctor Brougher quoted from an introduction written by Rogers for *Trails Plowed Under,* a book of reproductions of paintings of Charles M. Russell, the cowboy painter. Russell was dead when the book appeared in print. It was probably one of the finest things Rogers ever wrote.

"I guess you'll be able to set around now and chin with Mark Twain and James Whitcomb Riley and lots of them old joshers," he wrote. Then he went on wistfully to assume that heaven was a range with a good "chuck" wagon and plenty of food at nightfall. As though he were writing a letter directly to Russell he asked "Charley" to look around heaven and see if he could find Will's father and mother. He then concluded with "and if you see a little rascal running around, kiss him for me. Well, can't write you any more, Charley, dam paper's all wet. It must be raining in the bunk house." The "little rascal" was Will's boy, Fred, named after Fred Stone. He died in infancy.

Among those in the church were Stepin Fetchit, who played in pictures with Will, Eddie Cantor, the Stones, Clarke Gable, Spencer Tracy, Mary Pickford, Charlie Chaplin, Irvin Cobb, Walt Disney, and more than 100 others of Rogers' closest friends. Four Indians from Oklahoma came in a dilapidated car with cards inviting them to attend the private services in the church for their friend.

MEMORIAL SERVICES DRAW CROWD

Held simultaneously with the private services, a public memorial program was conducted in the Hollywood Bowl, where 25,000 persons gathered. The program was under the sponsorship of Hollywood civic organizations.

The crowd began assembling before noon, many of the early arrivals having come to the bowl after viewing the casket in Forest Lawn.

The program began with a two-minute silence, after which an American Legion band played "Nearer, My God, to Thee." Dr. Frank C. McKean, president of the Hollywood Ministerial Association, delivered the invocation, and was followed by Dr. Roy L. Smith, pastor of the First Methodist Church here.

The band played Beethoven's funeral march, and Conrad Nagel, film actor, delivered a reading. Lawrence Tibbett sang "By a Bier Side," from a poem by John Masefield.

Rupert Hughes, novelist and close friend of Rogers, delivered the eulogy, speaking extemporaneously.

Mr. Hughes declared that Rogers "rode the range of our American political life, taking care of those who would take from us our liberties."

"The first thing a despot does is to stifle and throttle laughter," Mr. Hughes added. "A dictator in this country would have a hard time with Rogers present.

"God send us some successor to Will Rogers, because we need someone to keep us laughing, as we must to save our dignity."

A third memorial service, marked by rites as unostentatious as Will Rogers himself, took place at the philosopher's own church, the Community Presbyterian Church in Beverly Hills, as 400 fellow-members of the congregation gathered to pay their last respects.

Dr. R. M. Donaldson, retired pastor of the church, led the service, taking as his theme "The Simplicity of Will Rogers."

It was Rogers who conceived the idea of building the church in 1921 and it was there that his three children received their first religious instruction.

"For Will Rogers the book is closed, but the life is not ended," Dr. Donaldson said. "There was a large and fascinating simplicity in Rogers' life. This pertained to his personal and family life, to his acting, to his writing, and to his friendship. Will Rogers sat on a throne never occupied by any other man in the hearts of the people. There was an atmosphere of friendship around Will that made his death a personal loss for all the world."

Meanwhile, the film industry paid its greatest tribute to one of its individual members. From two until three in the afternoon not a wheel turned in any studio. A few, forced by production schedules, reopened later in the afternoon, while others remained closed.

It was one of the rare occasions in theatrical history when the time-honored watchword, "The show must go on," was forgotten.

Memorial services were conducted at all the studios. At Twentieth Century Fox, where Rogers worked and where just a few brief days ago he waved a cheery good-by as he started northward to join Wiley Post, more than 3,000 studio workers and executives gathered to pay him honor.

On a huge sound stage the Rev. Josiah Hopkins, pastor of the Country Church of Hollywood, conducted a prayer for the departed actor, Colonel Jayson Joy, studio executive, voiced the sentiments of Rogers's fellow workers in a brief eulogy.

TRIBUTE PAID TO WILEY POST

At Oklahoma City, flowers dropped from the sky as the State paid tribute to Wiley Post. A throng of 15,000 persons almost got out of control at the Capitol Building where the bronze casket lay in state for more than two hours as the bier was removed to the church for the final obsequies.

Airplanes trailing crape streamers circled lazily, high above the building during the morning as the unnumbered multitude walked in rapid file past the bier.

Probably never before had there been a greater swarm of humanity here than that which jammed the corridors and entrances and extended many blocks beyond the building. A dozen women fainted and two nurses were assigned to care for them. National Guardsmen managed the throng with difficulty.

At noon, while thousands still awaited an opportunity for a last look at the flier's face, the State's official observance began. Governor Marland, accompanied by Brig. Gen. H. W. Butner of Fort Sill,

Sergeant Stanley R. Morgan, Point Barrow radio operator, who recovered the bodies of Will Rogers and Wiley Post and who flashed the news to the world.

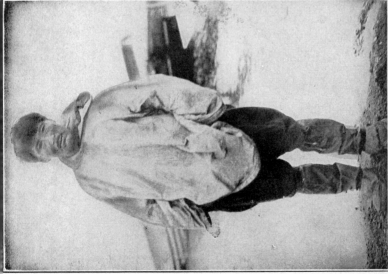

Through mist and fog, Clair Oakpeha, Eskimo, brought the news of the airplane crash to Point Barrow.

International News Photos, Inc.

The family of Will Rogers, as they started for Los Angeles. Left, Miss Theda Blake, sister of Mrs. Rogers; James Rogers, Mary Rogers, Mrs. Rogers, and Will Rogers, Jr.

representing President Roosevelt, marched through a forced lane to the second floor, where the body lay.

"Wiley Post has come to rest," the Governor said, his deep voice raised above the murmur of the crowd.

"The body of Oklahoma's son begins the sleep eternal beneath the sod he loved. His spirit, in company with the spirit of Oklahoma's Will Rogers, his pal, takes its flight to that bourne from which no traveler ever returns.

"Wiley Post flew around the earth. Wiley Post ascended above the earth to heights thought unattainable by man. Today Wiley Post precedes us, his friends, on that greater journey we all must take some day.

"Happy landing, Wiley Post, in that haven of all brave souls. Nothing we poor mortals can say or do will add to the lasting glory or prestige of these two Oklahoma sons.

"At this hour, at this moment, the people of this State, the people of the United States everywhere, pause in their earthly tasks or pleasures to do them honor.

"We who are assembled here, their Oklahoma kinsmen and friends, can say to our dear departed:

"Fare thee well, Will Rogers; fare thee well, Wiley Post.

"Happy landing!"

All was quiet, save the faint drone of the airplanes.

After a brief invocation by the Rev. William Slack, former naval airman and now minister of the Methodist Church at Lawton, the casket was moved toward the south steps of the Capitol.

When the Guardsmen bearing it walked into the sunshine, the planes dipped low, dropping wreaths and letting fall the somber streamers they had flown.

The crowd rushed to snatch up the blossoms and then surged toward the hearse. Police lines were broken as the thousands pressed toward the hearse, and the vehicle made its way toward the church with difficulty.

From the Capitol the crowd hurried to the First Baptist Church for the final rites at two o'clock in the afternoon after which the body was interred in a crypt at Fairlawn Cemetery.

CHAPTER XIV

SIDELIGHTS OF WILL ROGERS

THE LITTLE human-interest stories told about Will Rogers are almost countless. Everyone that knew him had dozens they could relate. All of them displayed some one of the many facets that went to make the humorist the great man that he was.

Rogers was "Bill" to brother members at the Friars Club. Friar Joe Laurie tells the following about him:

"Bill and I were discussing after-dinner speaking, of which he was one of the best. I asked him when and where his first speech was ever made. 'At the Y. M. C. A.—when I was a kid,' said Bill. 'I complained about the shower baths.'"

* * *

"I strolled into the library of the Friars Club one day and caught Bill reading a book. 'What are you reading, Bill?' I asked. 'I was just reading the Constitution of the United States and I was surprised to find out how many rights the people really have!' answered Bill."

* * *

"Bill and Frank Hawks, while making their tour through Arkansas giving concerts and raising money for the drought victims, were in an automobile making a trip from the flying field to the local convention hall, where they were to appear. The roads were bad and the car got stuck. A native passed by and they asked him if he would help them out. The native with a surly look answered 'No!' and drove on. Rogers turned to Hawks and said: 'If that is the milk of human kindness, I will take mine from a cow!'"

* * *

"The Prince of Wales, who was a great personal friend of Will Rogers, was making a trip to Africa on a good will and a hunting expedition. Someone asked Rogers whether it was true that the Prince was really going. 'Sure,' said Bill, 'the Prince is going to shoot wild animals as fast as they come out of their cages.'"

PROSPERITY RETURNS

Rogers predicted the return of prosperity on October 29, 1932, when arriving in New York, he said:

"Flew here today from Florida. Was going to stop in Washington, but the newspaper boys told me there wasn't a soul there."

"Ain't Mr. Hoover there?"

"No, he has gone to save Indiana."

"Well, I know my old Injun friend Charlie Curtis is here."

"No, he is saving Kansas."

"Well, then, I will just drop up and see some of the boys in the Cabinet."

"Why, there is none of the Cabinet; that's been gone since early in the spring."

"Well, who's running the country?"

"Why, nobody; that's why things are kinder picking up."

SOAK THE RICH

Another of his jibes in 1932 at the spending attitude of our legislators is reflected in a dispatch that purported to be "the diary of a U. S. Senate trying to find $2,000,000,000 that they have already spent but didn't have." It read:

"Monday—Soak the rich.

"Tuesday—Begin hearing from the rich.

"Tuesday afternoon—Decide to give the rich a chance to get richer.

"Wednesday—Tax Wall Street stock sales.

"Thursday—Get word from Wall Street: 'Lay off us or you will get no campaign contributions.'

"Thursday afternoon—Decide we are wrong about Wall Street.

"Friday—Soak the little fellow.

"Saturday morning—Find out there is no little fellow. He has been soaked until he is drowned.

"Sunday—Meditate.

"Next week—Same procedure, only more talk and less results."

A HORSE LAUGH

A corner of New York that was one of Will's favorites was East Twenty-fourth Street, near Lexington Avenue. A horse market was held there in those days and the neighborhood was studded with saddlers' and blacksmiths' shops.

One day an apparently broken-down nag was put up at auction. Nobody wanted the animal. Will strolled in just as the auctioneer was about to order the horse taken away.

"Twenty dollars," the comedian sang out.

"Sold!" cried the delighted auctioneer.

The teaming contractors and horse dealers grinned slyly, winked at each other, as the awkward-looking Westerner bought the animal which none of them would have taken as a gift.

Will sent the horse to Oklahoma to be put out to pasture. In a year the animal had rounded into flesh and strength. A breeder of hackneys offered him $2,000 for it.

"Nope, he ain't for sale," Rogers said. "I'm keeping him as a souvenir of New York—the big town where the wise guys come from."

That horse lived to round out his days on the lush acres of the Rogers rancho and in his time begat many a son and daughter that brought fancy figures. It was one of Will's few real-life experiences in a David Harum rôle—a character he was to play on the screen years later.

ONE ON McADOO

It was at Ziegfeld's informal entertainments that Will for the first time began to develop a reputation for spontaneous wit. The cabaret style of entertainment drew the same patrons to the "Midnight Frolic" night after night, and there was necessity for variety in his jokes. But that did not faze Will.

Accordingly, he kept up with current events and changed his "gags" daily to fit the trend in the news. Eventually habitual patrons would interrupt to ask him to comment on specific subjects. Sometimes they engaged in repartee from the floor, and Will had to be on his toes constantly.

He was equal to it. Gradually his mind quickened into the infallible mechanism which never failed him, on stage or off, for an epigram or a rejoinder.

Even in the Follies, he would indulge in his impromptu fun, and some nights he spotted personalities in the audience and singled them out for his jokes. Once he saw William G. McAdoo from the stage and requested the gentleman from California to leave his seat and come up behind the footlights.

McAdoo hesitated, but Will insisted and, finally, blushing profusely, he climbed up beside the comedian and stood blinking in the spotlight.

"Really," stammered McAdoo, "I thought I was through with politics."

"You are," drawled Rogers—and the audience roared.

DON'T SAY AIN'T

A friend met him after a long absence and invited him to dinner. "No, thanks," Will answered, "I've already et."

His friend corrected: "You shouldn't say 'et'; you should say 'have eaten.'"

Rogers grinned and drawled: "Well, I know a lot of fellers who say 'have eaten' who ain't et!"

A WORD OF ADVICE

Congressman William P. Connery, Jr., Democrat, of Massachusetts, told of the time when he and Rogers appeared on the same vaudeville stage at Rochester, N. Y., in 1910.

"Rogers had a favorite story to encourage other actors," said Connery. "It went like this:

"When I first got a vaudeville job, I had four horses. I dropped one horse and got more money. Then I dropped another horse and got a raise. Finally I dropped all the horses and I'm getting more money now that I ever did."

BEVERLY HILLS' PIONEERS

Reminiscing with his neighbors, Will Rogers said, "We lived out here in the early days with nothing but bean fields around us. When ground is so poor that nothing will grow, beans will flourish and many travelers used to come out here to watch the beans grow.

"We lived next to a vacant lot and a family began moving in. We were putting up a wire fence and, learning that the new neighbor was a lawyer, we put two barbed wires on top of the fence.

"I don't like to say it's the best, but Beverly Hills is one of the best known towns in the world. It is one of the early California settlements, settled about 1914. It was nothing in those days but a bean field and not good navy beans but just butter beans. Hollywood was breaking records both in production and scandal and many motion-picture people moved out here because they didn't want their neighbors to see who they were entertaining.

"Beverly Hills was settled by renegade actors from Hollywood. About 1919 was the real-estate slump, and the restrictions were removed, and that is when I came in. The town has gone along wonderful. You know we had splendid times in the old days. The town was just going along fine when somebody wanted to incorporate it and have bonds and a City Council. Then they started to degenerate and when they got the City Council, they started loans that put second mortgages on most homes.

"We got along great and have a wonderful police force and a jail. Our chief, you know, won't arrest any of our citizens. We had a little bad luck when the police caught John Gilbert and put him in jail. Since then nobody will go in it.

"In the early days, we had no churches. Now we have plenty of churches but no congregations.

"Then we all put in $500 to build a drug store and a grocery store. If you think this town has always been well-to-do, try to find out what became of that $500.

"The town has grown until it is known all over the country. I think it is one of the best little towns in the United States, but I hope it won't get too good."

Will Rogers shrewdly estimated the persons who pushed forward out of every crowd and clamored to meet him when he observed:

"Feller comes up and says, 'I see all your pictures.' I ask him which ones and he can't name one.   Woman brings up a little five-year-old girl and says 'Tillie wants to meet you.   She reads all your articles in the papers and enjoys them.'   Tilly says, 'Who is he, ma?' "

* * *

Will Rogers bred some fine polo ponies, but when wealthy players sought to buy any of them, he referred them to the cowboys, who worked around the movie lots.   He did that, it was said, so the boys, some of whom he trouped with in Wild-West days, could run up the prices and make something on the sale.

* * *

At a reception given by the National Press Club in Washington, Rogers was named "Congressman-at-large" and presented with a scroll attesting to this high and hitherto unheard-of office.   His duties were "to roam the country, pry into the state of the Union, check upon prohibition enforcement."   His tenure of office was to continue "during good behavior" and the job carried "a suspended salary of $1 a year."

THE WINNER

For many years Will Rogers always could be counted upon to dig down in his pocket and provide extra prize money for the contestants at the annual rodeo in Madison Square Garden.   Having taken part in many similar contests, he knew how the "boys" needed the money.   One year, however, he announced that he had his own idea for a contest and that he alone would be the judge.

He asked that "Maverick," a wild-eyed stallion, be led out.   He then proceeded to give the animal a rhinestone-studded feed bag as the champion "wild" horse of the show.

"You fellers," he told the riders, "have been gettin' paid for the animals' work for years.   It's about time one of the nags got a break."

At the same time, however, he put up his usual amount of money for extra prizes.

BETTER TIMES

Shortly before the flight to the Arctic, someone called attention to the fact that Rogers' fan mail was greatly increased over the preceding year.

"Signs of better times," said Will.   "More people have money to throw away on postage stamps."

SUGGESTS CUP FOR LIPTON

Sir Thomas Lipton, that gallant Irish sportsman, who tried for so many years unsuccessfully to bring the America's Cup back to England, found only sympathy from Rogers.   After the last of Lipton's *Shamrocks* was defeated, Rogers suggested that everybody send a dollar to Mayor Walker at New York to buy Lipton a bigger cup than the one he would have received if he had won.

Rogers said the cup should carry the inscription: "To possibly the world's worst yacht builder but absolutely the world's most cheerful loser.   You have been a benefit to mankind, Sir Thomas."

The suggestion was carried out by Mayor Walker.

FOREIGN AFFAIRS

Commenting on various foreign situations at different times Rogers said:

"I just wanted to see whether Trotsky ate, drank, slept, and laughed like a human or whether his whole life was taken up for the betterment of mankind."

On the Chino-Japanese war, Rogers humorously drew this conclusion: "Nobody knows what they are fighting about. It's almost like a European war in that respect."

*   *   *

His observations of English customs and American tourists were amusing:

"England has more money invested in dress suits and dinner jackets than America has plows and farming utensils. It is open season now in Europe for grouse and Americans; they shoot the grouse to put them out of their misery."

DOCTOR OF APPLESAUCE

The Oklahoma City University once considered offering Will Rogers an honorary degree of Doctor of Letters, one of the highest degrees. Will gleefully replied:

"What are you trying to do, make a joke out of college degrees? They are in bad enough repute as it is, without handing 'em around to comedians. The whole honorary degree thing is hooey.

"I saw some college giving Mellon one, and he is a billion bucks short. I got too much respect for people that work and earn 'em to see 'em handed around to every notorious character."

And modest, great Will concluded:

"My limit is a plain A.D., doctor of applesauce from the Oologah (Okla.) kindergarten."

FIRST POLITICAL SPEECH

In 1922, Rogers was asked by Kermit Roosevelt to make a Congressional election speech for Ogden Mills, a Republican. Will, a life-long Democrat, delivered some of his best quips, but Mills never even smiled. Rogers said, in part:

"I have spoken in all kinds of joints, from one of Mrs. Vanderbilt's parties to Sing Sing in Ossining, but this is my first political speech and I hope it flops. I don't want it to go over and then have to go into politics, because up to now I've always tried to live honest.

"A great many think I was sent here by Mr. Mills's opponent. This is not the case. I don't know him, but he must be a scoundrel. From what I have read of politics, every opponent is. He must also be a tool of the interests. I believe the least you can do is to say that in a political speech.

"Mr. Mills is quite a novelty. He is one of the few men that didn't go into politics from necessity. He was wealthy when he started.

"He is the only Congressman we can send to Congress who can go into a Fifth Avenue home without delivering something."

WISECRACKS

In his film, *Life Begins at Forty*, Rogers declared: "Hen eggs is more popular than duck eggs because a hen cackles to advertise her product." "If them quintuplets [the Dionnes] was born in this country, two of 'em would have to be plowed under. These days and times, nobody's got a right to be old folks."

A JOKE ON ROGERS

In the moving picture, *Life Begins at Forty*, Will Rogers found himself confronted with a situation about which he could not think of one of his ready answers. The situation of the story was a newspaper office conducted by Rogers, and the proofreader took him to task for misspelling so many words. Rogers accused the scenarist, Lamar Trotti, of "framing him."

HELP WANTED

One day in the studio restaurant, Rogers overheard Alice Faye describe a friend as "the silliest man" she ever met because he laughed at everything.

"Better give me his name," interrupted Rogers. "He'd be a good man for me to try out my jokes on."

GIVES ROCKEFELLER A DIME

Rogers turned the tables on John D. Rockefeller at Ormond Beach, Florida, in 1927, while playing a round of golf with the aged oil multi-millionaire. Rockefeller for many years had made a practice of passing out shiny, new dimes as presents on his birthday. Rogers started in to make Rockefeller smile.

"Is it true, Mr. Rockefeller," asked Rogers, "that every time you lose a golf match the price of gasoline goes up a cent."

Rockefeller was thoroughly amused at that one but a few minutes later Rogers made him laugh when he solemnly presented the oil magnate with a dime after the latter had made an exceptionally good shot.

"GIVE 'EM BAD ADVICE"

Charles Lathrop Pack, president of the American Tree Association, told how Rogers gave him advice in handling an educational campaign in tree planting.

"Will Rogers told me," said Pack, "that I was on the wrong track in trying to educate people to the value of putting idle land to work growing trees. 'Pack,' he said, 'you go down to Washington and get Congress to pass a law prohibiting tree planting and you'll have everybody doing it in a week.'"

CORN DOCTOR ROGERS

When Will Rogers finished the filming of Irvin S. Cobb's masterpiece, *Judge Priest*, the comedian was presented with a traveling kit. He looked at it and observed:

"This thing looks to me like a corn doctor's layout. I've always wanted to be a corn doctor, and now that I'm traveling over to Russia and Poland I wish some of the movie producers here present would give me letters to their relatives and friends back there so's I can do some business with 'em. Just give me a list of your families and I'll call on 'em and tell 'em how you're doin', and then I'll sell 'em corn plasters."

MEETS MUSSOLINI

When he met Mussolini, Will Rogers grinned.

"Interview?" asked Mussolini.

"No interview," declared Mr. Rogers.

"Hurray, bravo, no interview!" shouted Mussolini, and he sat down with the cowboy comedian and laughed at his jokes.

PUNCTURING A BALLOON

Will Rogers was against the inflationary measures that were proposed by New Deal politicians under President Franklin D. Roosevelt and once declared:

"We will never get anywhere with our finances till we pass a law saying that every time we appropriate something, we got to pass another bill along with it stating where the money is coming from."

A HELPING HAND

When the Friars Club, of New York, of which he was one of the leading members, lost their famous club house "The Monastery," on West Forty-eighth Street, New York, a movement was set on foot to get a donation of $500 from each of the wealthier members of the club. He wrote:

"It is worth $500 to see my brother members playing pinochle on the street. On second thought it is worth $500 to get them off the street."

He inclosed a check for $1000.

IN SOCIETY COLUMN

The society column of the newspaper in Rogers, Arkansas, carried the following social note in November 26, 1908, about Rogers' marriage:

"Miss Betty Blake and Will Rogers, of Claremore, Oklahoma, were married this afternoon at 1 o'clock by the Rev. J. G. Bailey at the home of the bride's mother, Mrs. A. J. Blake, in East Walnut Street."

ADVICE ON FOREIGN POLICY

The Government's practice in 1932 of writing notes to Japan warning them "what not to do" caused Rogers to advise "that we had better quit or Japan will have all of China.

"Every time they get a note they take another town they hadn't thought of until our note gave them the idea," he added. "The way we got into the last war was through notes. We send so many, nations can't tell which one we mean. Our wars ought to be labeled 'Entered on account of too much penmanship.' "

CALCULATING CAL

Rogers delighted in poking fun at the President— whoever he was, he was Rogers' friend—and even mimicked the late Calvin Coolidge on a radio program:

"Cairo's a great place," he wisecracked. "I was the only tourist there who never went out to see the Sphinx—well, I've seen Cal Coolidge."

EASY EDUCATION

"They say children in kindergarten must play in order to get them to learn. What do you mean, children?

"Cross-word puzzles learned grown folks more words than school teachers. And what arithmetic the womenfolks know they got at a bridge table. Our splendid English comes from attending the movies. My geography comes from an airplane window. Yes, sir, there is 120 million in the American kindergarten."

FOUL BALL

Rogers and Fred Stone appeared at a civic banquet, put on in Los Angeles to inspire a revival of interest in baseball. For an hour they held a great crowd of diners spellbound. Rogers imitated Stone's dances and Stone did Rogers' rope stuff.

At the end of the act, Rogers returned to his seat to find it occupied by a man who was urging the toastmaster to let him make a speech. He had dined not wisely but too well and was inclined to argue when Rogers suggested that he was in the wrong seat.

Rogers waved to the floor of the banquet hall and said with his infectious grin, "I'm playing this base, your're out in center field."

BULL'S EYE

I wonder if this Abyssinian king could sue and get his dues back that he has paid into the League of Nations for protection.

* * *

I bet you that history don't record any two nations ever having war with each other unless they had a conference first.

* * *

There ain't but one word wrong with every one of us in the world and that's selfishness.

I bet any Sunday could be made as popular at church as Easter is if you made them into fashion shows, too.

* * *

One of his favorite sayings was, "It's a great country but you can't live in it for nothing."

* * *

After Queen Marie had concluded her tour of the United States, he ruminated that "there is a fortune to be made for the person that can make something out of slightly used Rumanian flags."

* * *

Commenting upon the investigation of Mayor Walker of New York, he said that:

"No man was ever so investigated on one hand and dined on the other.   He keeps three decorations ahead of the investigating committee.   France gave 'Jimmie' Walker the Legion of Honor because he didn't bring nineteen other Mayors with him."

* * *

Congressional investigations are for the benefit of the photographers.

DANDRUFF

Irvin S. Cobb, the famous author, once cracked a joke at Rogers' expense, but from then on he feared the revenge that might follow and always asked to be called upon to speak at dinners after Will had delivered his speech.   The occasion was at a Friars Club dinner where Will Hays, the movie Czar, had paid tribute to Rogers by saying:

"They call New York a cold, heartless giant. But it has true appreciation of true and real worth.

When Will first blew in, an Oklahoma cowboy with a rope in his hand and a wad of chewing gum in his mouth, it didn't take New York long to find there was something under the old black cowboy slouch hat besides hair."

Cobb couldn't resist the opportunity. He jumped up, and said:

"I'm deeply touched by what Mr. Hays just said because it's high time in this country that someone is speaking a kind word about dandruff."

HOME TOWN STUFF

Will was once urged to go back to Oklahoma City and give a show in an armory, which seated 10,000 persons.

"But I'm not going," says Rogers. "Not back there where they all know me. Why they'd say, 'Will's just talking the way he used to on the street corner round here. Old Cap Stallings can talk more than that. This is no show.' "

T. R. IDEAL AUDIENCE

Theodore Roosevelt was Rogers' notion of the ideal audience. "I never got him into the theater but I gave him a couple of private shows and he liked them and laughed. And when I got all done, he said: 'That's fine, but go ahead now and do the jokes you tell about me.' "

INTRODUCING LADY ASTOR

One night Lady Astor was in the audience at the Follies and Rogers asked her if she would stand up. She did so graciously.

"When I played in London," Rogers said, "I used to visit Lady Astor at the House of Parliament. When she came to see me when I was playing over there, I tried to get her to stand up and take a bow. She always refused. Yet every time I went to see her in the House of Parliament, they could never get her to sit down."

ON FIRST-NIGHTERS

Will Rogers was convinced that the average first-night audience on Broadway didn't keep abreast of current events, as he tried out many of his gags on them only to have them fall flat.

"They know about boots and shoes and automobiles," Rogers once remarked, "but they don't read the newspapers. Next season, I won't appear on the first night. I'll show the second night."

But a first night of the Follies without Rogers wouldn't have been much of a success.

FROM THE FOLLIES

On the opening night of the Follies of 1918, Will Rogers cleverly summed up the new show in the following way:

"It's a great thing to see the Follies on its first night, because by the time you get back to your homes in the Bronx, a lot of the show will be in Cain's theatrical storehouse along with a bunch of my jokes.

"A first night of the Follies is a great function. Everyone brings his new wife to see his old one act. You see, we had quite a lot of trouble keeping our

v

girls together on tour. Every town we went to some of them would marry a millionaire, but in a few weeks they would be divorced and catch up with the show again.

"Women are like elephants. I like to look at 'em but I'd hate to own one."

WAR-TIME STUFF

The World War furnished Rogers with a lot of his stage material.

"The United States is going to be much more severe with the German spies that are captured in the future. We're going to put their names in the papers.

"We're getting a lot of actors in the army. I heard the other day that George M. Cohan was going to join the nasal brigade. I read in the paper that President Wilson made another speech. I suppose Congressmen will come along now and misunderstand him. It must be awful hard for a smart man like the President to make a speech in such a way that a bonehead Congressman and a highbrow mail carrier will both get what he means."

A HUMORIST'S CATECHISM

Will Rogers once derived considerable fun from writing out his own questions and answers on the subject of humor. Some of them read:

"What's the best way to start being a humorist?"

"Recovery from a mule kick is one way that's used a lot. Being dropped head downward on a pavement in youth has been responsible for a lot.

But a discharge from an asylum for mental cases is almost sure fire."

"Is the field of humor crowded?"

"Only when Congress is in session."

"What talent is necessary? Must one be born with a funny bone in his head?"

"It's not talent, it's an affliction. If a funny bone is necessary, I would say that in the head is the best place to have it. That's the least used of a humorist's equipment."

HIS FAVORITE DISH

The gilded lobster palaces of the Broadway playboys had no charm for Rogers when he was starring in the Ziegfeld Follies. He preferred a little "hole-in-the-wall" restaurant where they had, in his opinion, the best chile peppers and chile con carne in New York. It is at Seventh Avenue and Forty-seventh Street and he went there almost nightly, sitting on one of the white stools at the little counter to eat his chile. The place is called El Rancho and is owned by a Swede, named Arvid Strom. The nationality of the proprietor always gave Will a laugh. He could not reconcile that fellow being the proprietor of a Mexican cafe that sold chile con carni.

"A Swede running a chile joint," he once said, "that's a great gag."

In those days Rogers was getting $500 for personal appearances at banquets and he told Strom, "I can only make those speeches by eating chile before and after."

MEETING WITH MDIVANIS

When Rogers first met the Mdivani brothers, Princes David and Serge, whose matrimonial experiences were varied, he wisecracked:

"Well, boys, I am happy to meet you—but don't ask me to marry you."

HIS VERY FIRST MOVIE

Will Rogers' first experience before the motion-picture camera actually took place six years before he went on the movie lots. In 1912 a deer drive was organized at Shelter Island after the animals had caused havoc in gardens there. One of those taking part in the drive was Will. He was knocked down by a buck and later found a small fawn. A news-reel camera man asked Rogers to pose with the young animal in his arms.

RECOMMENDATION

What the Red Cross thought of Will Rogers was shown in a telegram made public after the humorist's death. It was sent to him in 1933 by John Barton Payne, then head of that organization. It read:

"When I pass from the Red Cross and knock at St. Peter's gate, he will ask, 'Who comes here?'

"I will answer, 'John Barton Payne, chairman of the American Red Cross.'

"He will ask, 'By what right do you expect to enter?'

"I will answer, 'I knew Will Rogers.'

"He will say, 'That is sufficient. Come right in.'"
Payne died in January, 1935.

WINNING A BET FROM LINDBERGH

On the opening of *Three Cheers* in New York, Will Rogers won a wager from Colonel Charles A. Lindbergh. Lindbergh knew that Rogers took great delight in calling on celebrities to stand up and be introduced to the house. The famous flier asked Rogers not to introduce him, and in joking about it Lindbergh bet the comedian he would not be able to resist the temptation.

"It was the hardest bet I ever won in my life," Rogers declared.

POLITICAL ADVICE

The worst thing Alfred E. Smith ever did in his campaign for President, in the opinion of Will Rogers, was to wear a brown derby.

"It would have been better," he told a group at the Friars Club, "if Al had worn overalls and a hay hat. That derby made him look like a city slicker."

ONLY SENATORS

One day Rogers was engaged in one of his favorite pastimes, "gabbing," with a couple of stage hands in the New Amsterdam Theater. The doorman came up and said: "Mr. Rogers, there are a couple of Senators waiting at the door for you."

"Oh, let 'em wait a minute," Rogers replied. "They're only Senators."

A GRACEFUL GESTURE

Will Rogers by a simple act of thoughtfulness saved the annual dinner of the Academy of Motion-Picture Arts and Sciences in 1934 from being turned into an anti-climax. Charles Laughton and Katherine Hepburn, who won the awards for 1933, were not able to be present.

Rogers called the four runners-up, Paul Muni, Leslie Howard, May Robson, and Diana Wynyard to the speakers' platform. After the 800 Hollywood notables present had applauded, Will presented each of the four with a rose from the bouquet in front of him.

A FEW STATISTICS

"How many times have I whirled a rope?" Rogers asked by way of answering a question. "Well, I roughly calculate that if the lariat was long enough and all the loops I've coaxed out of it could be made into one, it would pretty near circle this big globe of ours. The number of tons of chewing gum I've masticated while spinning monologs comes under the head of manufacturing statistics."

WHEN JOKES FAILED

Despite the fact that Rogers tried out his jokes on his family and others before presenting them on the stage, it sometimes happened that the audience would fail to find them mirth-provoking. For the average monologist that was a serious situation but Rogers knew how to handle it.

"When I tell a couple of jokes and there is only a ripple of laughter," he said, "I stall with the talk and get into heavy action with the rope. Then I give the audience the damnedest two minutes of rope swingin' you ever saw."

ROGERS AND HIS GUM

The eternal wad of gum that Rogers chewed upon the stage was only a part of the act, but one night on the New Amsterdam Roof he accidentally swallowed it in the midst of his monolog.

He gulped and then excused himself for a moment. He ran to his dressing room and procured another package of gum.

"I feel as conspicuous without my gum," he explained to the audience, "as a chorus girl in ankle-length skirts."

STRAIGHT FROM THE SHOULDER

One day when his audience at a lecture was made up largely of women, Will Rogers looked at them with a twinkle in his eye and declared:

"You women just prowl from one meeting to another. Each one of you ought to be home cookin' lunch instead of bein' here. Americans will join anything in town but their families. Why, two Americans can't meet on the street without one bangin' a gavel and calling the other to order."

COLLECTING THE PAY

In the early days with Zach Mulhall's Wild West, Rogers and Tom Mix were close friends. There were times when the circus owner had difficulty meeting the payroll. On such occasions, Rogers once related, Mulhall would go to the hotel bar and buy drinks for anyone in the place as a means of calling attention to his show.

"Tom and I were not invited to come over for a drink," said Mr. Rogers with his inimitable drawl. "We were only working for Colonel Mulhall. But we went just the same, and we framed up a way to get something out of the old showman. Zach would shout out, asking everybody to have a drink with him, and Tom and I watched the actions of the old man. We knew that sooner or later he would have to pay for the drinks, and when he pulled out a roll and peeled off a big bill, we edged up on each side of him, without giving him a chance to suspect what was going to happen. We had resolved that we would get some money somehow that night, and it was with relief that we saw Zach hand a twenty-dollar bill to the bartender. We waited for our chance, and the second the bartender put the change on the bar, our hands shot out and grabbed all of it, to Zach's grief and surprise."

GOAT ROPING LEADS TO POLO

How Will Rogers became a polo enthusiast was revealed by J. A. Wigmore, Cleveland millionaire and polo player, who taught the game to the humorist.

"In 1920 in Hollywood two cowboys became involved in an argument over which could rope and tie a goat in the shortest time," said Wigmore. "The result was a contest and when the day for the contest arrived, the side bet exceeded a thousand dollars.

"The affair was staged in Beverly Hills and Rogers, who threw a mean rope and was no slouch as a rider, challenged the winner. A few days later, Rogers telephoned me and asked permission to borrow a pair of cutting horses I had brought to Pasadena from my ranch in New Mexico.

"I lent them to him and Rogers easily won the goat-roping championship. The next day he telephoned me and said: 'I have no idea what price you might set on those horses, so I'm sending you a signed check. You fill it in, I've just got to have 'em.'

"I told him if the boys on the ranch found out I had sold those ponies, they'd never let me back on the ranch, adding that the only way I could square matters would be to make him a present of them.

"Rogers was reluctant to accept them, but he did and agreed to the condition imposed—that he would come out to Midwick and learn to play 'stick and ball.' He came, and soon he was crazy about the game."

NOT A CANDIDATE

In the days when Rogers was enjoying his great popularity as a citizen of California, a movement was started to have Will Rogers entered in the race for Governor of the State, but the gubernatorial boom ended as quickly as it started when he declared:

"I'm not a candidate for anything. I'd rather be a poor actor than a poor governor. After rawhiding these fellows for so many years, I'm satisfied to remain fancy free to go where I please when I please."

AT A LOSS FOR WORDS

Will Rogers' fame as a humorist was based upon the fact that he could be depended upon to say the unexpected right thing at the unexpected right moment. Owen D. Young once called him on the long-distance telephone and asked him to share a radio program with President Hoover in behalf of unemployment relief.

Fifteen minutes after talking with Young, a fellow actor found him sitting at the telephone staring into space.

"What's the matter, Bill?" the actor asked.

"Boy, I'm scared to death," he replied. "I've got to help Hoover make a speech."

GETTING AWAY WITH IT

A friend once asked Rogers how he managed to get by without getting into difficulty over his quips and jests about persons and things.

"I get by," he answered, "because I ain't for anything. I ain't selling anything. I ain't got a remedy for anything.

"It's easy to kid a big man, but you've got to look out for the little fellows. A big man'll take a joke on himself but you've got to be careful if his secretary is around.

"There are some awful silly people. I got the most ridiculous letter once from a girl. She said I was a Bolshevik, an anti-American, and a menace to the country because I made light remarks about our President.

"If a fellow doesn't have a good time once in a while and get a good laugh out of the serious side of life, he doesn't half live."

RANDOM SHOTS

"We stood through one speech," Rogers said of the London Naval Conference in 1930, "sat through eight and slept through twelve, and in three solid hours of compliments not a rowboat was sunk."

* * *

"You people," he told a crowd at Buenos Aires, "export meat, wheat, and gigolos and the United States puts a tariff on the wrong two."

* * *

When Andrew Mellon was named Ambassador to England, Rogers chirped: "Why, a man with as much money as Andy could be popular anywhere."

* * *

"The movie game is easier than it was. They used to have a terrible time getting actors to cry for the screen. Every actor cries now when he hears the salary he is going to get."

* * *

"A holding company is where you hand an accomplice the goods while a policeman searches you."

* * *

"They're as busy as usual passing appropriation bills like hot biscuits at a country farmhouse."

* * *

"One thing about farmers' relief. It can't last long, for the farmers ain't got much more to be relieved of."

WORRIES FATHER

After Will Rogers had begun to earn a little money as a vaudeville performer, his first thought was to show his father that he was on the road to success. He saved his money until he had $500 and then sent his father a draft for that amount. His father didn't need the money, and instead of being pleased, he became very suspicious of this queer business of his son's.

The old gentleman, then a member of the Oklahoma Constitutional Convention, showed the draft to William H. "Alfalfa Bill" Murray, who afterwards became a colorful Governor of that State.

"Do you think Willie made that money honestly?"

Murray, who related the story years later, assured the elder Rogers that the money was undoubtedly earned honestly.

OF EARLY VINTAGE

One of Rogers' earliest quips from the stage was carried on down through the years as one of his best. He was twirling a rope in a vaudeville show when during a lull he remarked carelessly to the audience:

"Swingin' a rope's all right—if your neck ain't in it."

The audience, taken by surprise, roared at the quip. Rogers later admitted he was surprised at the response.

NOTES ON RUSSIA

"They got a great idea over there in Russia. They divide everything up but nobody had anything to divide in the first place. Russian men wear their shirts hanging outside their pants. Any nation that don't know enough to tuck in their shirt tail will never get anywhere. Grammar and I get along like a Russian and a bathtub."

A CENTURY OF PROGRESS

In a radio address, Rogers used the Century of Progress in Chicago as a springboard to hurl a few criticisms at progress in general.

"That Century of Progress Exhibition is misnamed. I can't figure whether we made any progress in the last 100 years or not. I think they ought to call it 'What the last 100 years has done to us.' You take in 1833 we had only 36 Senators and the evil has grown now until we have 96, and did you know there wasn't such a thing as a stenographer in 1833. Every Congressman could write then.

"And 100 years ago we were on the gold standard, and 100 years ago Europe didn't owe us anything. We were smart enough to owe them. I tell you the older we get the dumber we get. Then you lived until you died and not until you were just run over."

GOVERNOR WANTED

Will Rogers once was asked to become one of the board of governors at the Friars Club and he declined because the movies required him to spend most of his time in Hollywood.

"If it's a humorist you want, there are any number of 'em in the club," he said. "If it's an actor you want, there's no end of good actors and there are plenty of newspaper men.   The only thing I can do that they can't is spin a rope.   If it's a governor you really want—there's Friar Al Smith."

* * *

Will Rogers always had a very humble opinion of himself.   Despite the plaudits that were accorded him; regardless of the continuous stream of gold that poured into his pockets; and, apparently, unmindful of the assurances of his closest friends, he never made any pretensions about himself or the high place he held in the world.   His own estimate of himself was:

"Shucks, I was just an old cowhand that had a little luck.   Why all this here fuss about me?"

CHAPTER XV

WILL ROGERS, THE MAN

THERE was only one Will Rogers. His generation never produced a man with such a wide variety of outstanding talents. His genius was unique and it led him on to where he was sought by Princes and Presidents, but he always remained the plain, unassuming man to whom a lowly stage hand was just as important as a powerful statesman. Fortune and world fame were his, yet he always kept his sharp-heeled cowboy boots firmly on the ground. The motion pictures, radio, the printed word and the stage were used by him as a medium of conveying his thoughts to others and made his name a household word of tremendous influence. A tireless traveler, he found his material in many lands but never did he forget his beginning on a cattle ranch in the old Indian Territory. He was at once a cowboy, rodeo rider, comedian, philosopher, humorist, and philanthropist, and his career seems almost fabulous. He might have been half a dozen men so many were his talents. Through all the plaudits that came his way he remained humble, always creating the impression that the applause was not meant for him. That was no pose with Will Rogers.

ROGERS' HUMILITY

His humility was the sincerest thing about him. After years on the stage, before the motion-picture camera, and behind the microphone he doubted his ability as an actor. In the picture, *Steamboat Round the Bend,* released about the time of his death, Rogers went to Ben Burman and said:

"Ben, you've got a grand yarn here and I like my part, but I am afraid that I'm not going to be able to play it the way it ought to be done."

The statement probably never was made before in Hollywood—the world's capital of egocentrics.

He frequently claimed he was "no actor." He didn't have to be. The character of Will Rogers was what the millions wanted to see and they gave their hearty approval.

Rogers often expressed similar views about his studiously unlettered writings and jokes. He was far from unlettered and actually was a keen student of the complexities of international politics and economics.

"Most people think of me as a gag man," Will once said. "You have to be funny to keep 'em listenin' and readin'. I'm just an ignerant feller, without any education, so to speak, but I try to know what I'm talking about. I joke to the public, but I do a lot of studying because, although I hand out a lot of foolishness, I don't want to hand out stuff that might be misleadin'.

KNEW HIS AUDIENCE

"I read editorials a lot and while I'm reading them the thought comes to me that I can get this bit of news into the minds of the audience—only in a different way. When I go to a national convention

I have to know what they're talking about to know what's funny. If I was just a clown, Borah and Reed and Mellon and all those fellows wouldn't take the trouble to explain what they're drivin' at to me. I never worked harder in my life than at the London Disarmament Conference.

"I ain't for anything. I look at all of 'em and I laugh at all of 'em but I don't advocate. I haven't hardly any politics. Of course, I do belong to the Democratic party, but even the best of us has got to let a little cussedness come out now and then.

"It's a terribly hard job. The guys that tell you they can be funny at any minute, without any effort, are guys that ain't funny to anybody but themselves. I depend on the newspapers for most of my inspirations. Some days there is material for several good lines. Then there may be a week when there isn't a little thing worth mentioning. About once a month I turn out a gag that I get a big kick out of myself. That's a pretty good average.

"I try to outguess the people out in front. If I see a news event, something like the Armament Conference, I try to figure out what some particular part of it is going to develop into. I never had the slightest idea but what the Japanese would come out of that conference with more than they took into it. When I made remarks like that, my audience didn't get it at first."

Rogers' ideas on recreation were equally simple. He was of the theater yet he seldom went to a performance. Neither did he care for fishing and hunting.

RECREATIONS, RIDIN' AND ROPIN'

"My recreations," he once said, "are mostly ridin' and ropin'. I'd rather work out with the ranch boys. Once I went from California to Texas to help at an annual calf brandin'. Wrestlin' a big calf in the hot sun is some exercise. I remember one of the boys said: 'You sure have doggone queer ideas of a vacation.'

"Out in Hollywood I am regarded as an eccentric."

And yet when that "eccentric" died, the legislative machinery of the nation at Washington was stopped to pay him honor. Millions of words were printed about him all over the world. His words were recalled and it is doubtful if any man without rank or title was ever accorded the homage that was given him.

SENATE TRIBUTE

In the stately Senate chamber at the Capitol, Senator Joseph T. Robinson, of Arkansas, voiced the sentiment of the nation when the Senate convened the day after Rogers' death.

"Probably the most widely known citizen of the United States, and certainly the best beloved, met his death some hours ago in a lonely and faraway place," he said.

"We pause for a moment in the midst of our duties to pay brief tribute to his memory and that of his gallant companion. I do not think of Will Rogers as dead.

"I shall remember him always as a sensible, courageous, and loyal friend, possessed of unusual and notable talent. He made fun for all mankind. In nothing he ever said was there an intentional sting.

"He was kind, generous, and patriotic.] His companion was a courageous representative of a gallant group who on the wings of adventure sought remote places and conquered long distances.

"All the Nation mourns these great citizens. They were both representatives of the highest type of manhood.

"Peace to them."

JOHN McCORMACK

John McCormack, the famous singer, who once appeared with Rogers in the Follies for one performance for the benefit of the Mississippi River flood sufferers, sent the following expression of sorrow to the New York *Times:*

"Overwhelmed with grief, I send to you, sir, and through you to his dear ones, my most heartfelt sympathy in the tragic death of my dear friend, Will Rogers. A smile has disappeared from the lips of America, and her eyes are now suffused with tears. 'He was a man; take him for all in all, I shall not look upon his like again.'"

Tributes were paid to Rogers in all parts of the world and the great and near-great, many of whom had been targets for his darts of humor, saw only a great tragedy in his passing.

There were some who professed to see in Rogers during his life everything that he actually was not. It was only a small group of so-called intellectuals who found him irritating. But there was nothing they could do about it, for he turned around and everything he did was successful. When he wrote for the magazines every first-class periodical in the country wanted his work. In the movies his salary, it was reported, ranged between $300,000 and $500,000 a year. He tried his hand at polo and after learning the rudiments of the game was able to play with the best in the world. On the radio he received the highest pay on record for a single broadcast.

DEVOTED TO HIS FAMILY

Will Rogers was essentially a family man. His home, his wife and children were the greatest things in his life, but he was no autocrat there. With the children he played as if he were one of them, and whenever it was necessary to reprimand one of the youngsters he always found some excuse to leave the room at once and leave the disciplining to Mrs. Rogers.

The story is told of an old cowhand who worked on Will's ranch, a talkative, good-natured fellow named Pete, who had been hired to shoe horses and mules. Pete, it seems, had a pension adequate for his needs, and it was suggested that he be laid off. The matter was called to Rogers' attention several times but nothing happened.

"It's this way," said Rogers, when pressed for an explanation. "Jimmy (the youngest of the Rogers children) likes to sit and talk to the old man. When I find out what Pete does to earn his money around here. I'll fire him."

Pete left eventually, but not because he was fired.

Another incident that revealed the character of the man was the time one of his sisters had died in Oklahoma while he was playing in the Follies. By hard, weary riding, that was in the days before air travel, he reached the town in time for the funeral. As he entered the home he saw that the room was banked with flowers sent by the men and women in the show.

"They can't tell me about New York and show people," Rogers said on his return. "It's the grandest city and they're the grandest people in the whole world."

WILL AND DOROTHY STONE

On another occasion, Dorothy Stone, the daughter of his best friend, was visiting the Rogers ranch. Florenz Ziegfeld wanted to star her in *Show Girl* and he called Fred Stone to arrange an appointment. Stone told him his daughter was at Rogers' home.

Ziegfeld asked Stone to call her, and was told that Rogers would not allow a telephone on the ranch. Stone drove out there and it was arranged that Dorothy was to start east. In order that no time might be wasted, a manuscript of the play was sent to her by airplane.

The plane, however, was three hours late and Miss Stone had started before it arrived. Rogers seized the script, boarded an eastbound airplane, and flew after Miss Stone's train. He caught up with her at the first important railway stop and placed the script in her hands. It was all just a little fun for Rogers.

Still another phase of his wonderful character was shown after the turn of the year of 1934 when the United States took over the flying of the airmail. Rogers arrived in New York prepared to broadcast some humorous remarks on the airmail situation.

A few minutes before he went on the air, word was received that the commercial plane in which he had flown east had crashed, killing the two pilots and the hostess. He was stunned by the news. He requested that the audience which was to sit in the studio during his broadcast be dismissed and that he be given a small speaker's studio. He then went on the air and extolled the fliers. Tears were streaming down his cheeks when he finished.

NEVER DID A MEAN THING

Will Rogers never did an unkind thing. If he did, there is no record of it anywhere. Nor would he hit the fellow that was down.

"You folks know I never mean anything by the cracks I make here on politics," he once said on the stage. "I generally hit the fellow that is on top because it isn't fair to hit a fellow that is down. If a big man laughs at jokes on him, he's all right."

Rogers made his major emphasis on politics, and he was able to present his observations in quick, sure, and simple phrases. It was the sort of talk the average American might make if he had Will's great gift of humor. It was that quality that endeared him to the masses. Many looked upon him as the ideal American statesman and he was seriously suggested for every office from President down.

"There's already too many comedians in Washington," he laughed. "Competition would be too keen for me."

Rogers never forgot he was a plainsman and that he spoke the language of the common people. He was indifferent to rank and title. A man had to stand on his ability so far as Will was concerned. Only Will Rogers would have dared, as the principal speaker at a bankers' convention, to begin:

"You're as fine a group of men as ever foreclosed on a widow. I am glad to be with you Shylocks."

But this barbed shaft coming from Rogers was greeted with hearty laughter. They knew there was no venom in his heart.

TRUTH ABOUT ADVERTISING

Again at a dinner before advertising men he delivered what he described as a "message of truth about advertising. An advertising club, he told the men," was the Mother Lodge of Liars" and pleaded with them to let "a little truth creep into their copy." Will himself once wrote pithy sayings for advertising copy and assured his listeners he knew what he was talking about.

"You have members who write real-estate advertising," he said, "That's the post-graduate course in lying."

That Rogers was absolutely without any bluff or front was shown when he was invited to play polo with the Prince of Wales, during his visit to this country in 1924.   The game was played at the exclusive Piping Rock Club on Long Island.   The prince wore white polo breeches, a tan sweater, and the usual Indian pith helmet.   Rogers appeared in ordinary riding clothes with his customary leather jacket.   That he was not attired in correct polo clothing made no difference to Rogers nor to the Prince.   Whenever there was an exchange of ponies, the two seemed to drift together and most of the time the Prince laughed heartily at Rogers' remarks.

ROGERS DEFENDS THE PRINCE

Later Rogers stoutly defended the Prince's ability as a horseman.

"He's there and don't make any mistake about it," Rogers declared.   "He rides well and he rides horses that are hard to manage.

"I played only three chukkers against him.   It was one of those 'cut-in' games and everybody got a chance to play.   The Prince was well mounted. He knows good horseflesh when he sees it.   I was ridin' a coupla dogs.   One I could have got off and outrun myself.

"And while we're talkin' about ridin', don't forget those point-to-point races that fellow rides in England.   They aren't like cross-country affairs here with artificial fences that collapse if a horse touches them.   They have stone walls built by some king a million years ago for jumps.   If your horse hits one of them, you fall."

In China, while the United States Marines were

on duty there at Shanghai, he won the admiration of the "leathernecks" when he greeted them:

"Take me to the cabarets with the swinging doors you can kick open with your feet. I want to see the places our Marines enjoy themselves."

AVOIDS "STUFFY AFFAIRS"

While in China, he was deluged with invitations to attend many functions and he was kept busy avoiding what he described as "stuffy affairs."

"I want to spend my time in any place where I can talk with friendly people," he said, "and keep my hat on my head."

Rogers did not mind sharing the spotlight on one occasion with Oscar, head waiter at the Waldorf. Oscar was busy directing his corps of waiters as they hurried around serving 1,500 members of the Society of Automotive Engineers. Rogers called Oscar to the speakers' table and presented him to the gathering. The diners rose and applauded.

A short time later when Rogers rose to deliver the principal address of the evening, the diners also arose and applauded.

"Sit down," he commanded. "You'll tip over your bottles."

Rogers was referring to the fact that prohibition was in effect and that many of the diners who brought liquor to the dinner had the bottles on the floor at their feet.

Instead of "lambasting" the engineers, however, he said he "liked engineers because they looked like someone that was mindin' his own business."

SLAMS THE "JOINERS"

On a similar occasion when he was the principal speaker at a drive staged by a merchants association for new members he slammed all "joiners" with a yarn about a mythical old fellow in Oklahoma.

"Out in Oklahoma, where I live," he said, "there was an old fellow that worked in the oil wells and they said: 'John, are you goin' to join the Eagles?' 'Nope,' John answered, 'I am neither an Elk nor an Eagle nor a Shriner. I'm just goin' to remain an ordinary drunkard.'"

A man of lesser stature than Rogers would probably have been silenced right then and there but he had the faculty of delivering such jolts with a roguish grin that made his auditors take it and like it. He then went on to comment on world affairs.

HARD LUCK FOR TURKEY

"Turkey had some hard luck last week," he said. "They had a war all booked and it was canceled on them at the last minute. You know, you can't get a war with Turkey on a minute's notice. You have to book it way ahead.

"They look at their catalogs and tell you they are fighting in 1930. They have so many wars, they say like a baseball team: 'We lost five and won three and are still in the second division. Next year we'll go out and do better.'

"England got kind of sore because we did not join in with Turkey on this last war. We can't go into another war. We are two bonuses behind already.

"One of the speakers here today spoke of the achievements of this association under the heading of 'post-office department.' I see you have improved that in some way. I noticed the other day we had another mail robbery. That's one thing you never heard during the Democratic Administration. You had no mail robberies. Robbers never knew when the mail was coming."

The United States Senate, however, was always a shining mark for Will, and in one of his radio broadcasts he held a mock session of that august body to the huge delight of millions of listeners.

"The Senate of the United States will now come to order. It is fortunate that we are holding this session in this ballroom of this beautiful hotel to give a lot of you Senators a chance to get in here that never would have got in any other way.

THE NEW DEAL

"To show how the New Deal is working, there must be 1,500 people in the hall here. It gives you an idea of the unemployed that are here now. Mr. John Nance Garner, you just stay sitting right where you are in the front row. You'll have nothing to do with the running of this meeting. I am running this outfit here. I don't want you to go to sleep as usual, either, because this is one speech you haven't heard a hundred times. You've heard worse speeches but you never heard this one. After this meeting is over, I have some good news for you, you can go right back to your regular business. There's going to be a poker game as soon as this is over.

"Order in the court. I have just got a bill from the White House. We will have the usual pro= cedure with it. We won't read it. Nobody knows what it is and we'll vote for it in the usual way.

"All in favor say 'Aye' and those opposed say, 'No.' The 'ayes' have it. No, wait a minute. We have just a small gathering of Republican Sena- tors here. I'll fix a place over there for them in the pantry. Maybe a little later there'll be a few bankers that I'll have to put in with the Republi- cans, but you can watch them yourselves. You boys will set there and be quiet. I am sure that if you'll behave yourselves, the management won't make any holler about your being here. Wait a minute. I have just received another bill from the White House. There's something the matter They're coming awful slow today. We'll vote on this in the usual way. It won't be read. I don't know what it is. All those in favor say 'Aye;' all those opposed say, 'No.' The bill is passed."

AT DISARMAMENT CONFERENCE

That was Will Rogers. Presidents, Senators, and others in high office—none escaped his witticisms. Even King George once came in for some of his raillery. He prefaced his remarks with telling how he attended the Disarmament Conference in 1930 and heard King George make a speech.

"Some people go to baseball games, some go to other things," he said, "I go for my laughs and things just to Disarmament Conferences. When the King made his speech, here is something I will never forget. He stood in front of a chair and we all stood up during his speech. Then he walked out and we still stood.

"Then four men came in and carried out his chair. We didn't know what it was. Well, it was the Crown Chair. What happened was, he saw the American delegation sitting there. When he got outside, you know, he happened to think of this chair and think of this delegation and of the way Americans are always curio hunting, and he says, 'Boys, go back and get that chair, will you and bring it here?' I'll never forget that."

PRESIDENT SHOCKED BY TRAGEDY

Will Rogers, Ambassador of Good Will, was the only one who might have dared to be so flippant without arousing the criticism of King George's nation. But he was loved everywhere for that gentle humor that carried with it a breath of the honest soil from which he had sprung. The philosopher from the prairie lands left millions of friends behind.

What the passing of Will Rogers meant to the world was best exemplified by the expressions of profound sorrow that the great men he had known said of him.

"I was shocked," said PRESIDENT ROOSEVELT," to hear of the tragedy which has taken Will Rogers and Wiley Post from us. Will was an old friend of mine, a humorist and a philosopher beloved by all. I had the pleasure of greeting Mr. Post on his return from his round-the-world flight. Both were outstanding Americans and will be greatly missed.

Former PRESIDENT HOOVER said: "The news of the death in an airplane crash of Will Rogers and Wiley Post has come as a terrible shock to me. I have long known both of these fine Americans and have long been appreciative of their accomplishments. In origin and accomplishment they were typically American, with their careers appealing to everyone appreciative of the pioneer spirit. They were great souls and I feel a sense of deep personal loss in their passing."

GOVERNOR LEHMAN of New York, said: "I am deeply shocked and grieved to hear the terrible news. Will Rogers and Wiley Post were outstanding figures in American life. I greatly admired both of them. Probably no men in America had more friends and admirers than they. The whole country will mourn their tragic death."

GOVERNOR MARLAND of Oklahoma: "The State will want to give them a memorial, but the State can't add anything to the honors already heaped upon them by the sovereigns and people of the world."

MOST POPULAR MAN OF HIS TIME

EDDIE CANTOR: "Will Rogers was probably the most beloved man of our time. He was one man in the entertainment world who more than balanced by his exemplary life any of the scandals involving people of the theatre. He was the most charitable, most tolerant man I have ever known. There wasn't an atom of envy in his system."

BILLIE BURKE: "He was one of the kindest men and best friends in the world. I have known him for many years from the day he was just starting out in the Follies. When my husband passed away, Mr. Rogers was like a brother to me."

SAMUEL GOLDWYN: "I have lost a great friend. The stage and screen have lost a great artist. America has lost her greatest humorist since Mark Twain. I am too deeply affected to say more."

WILL H. HAYS: "It does not take time to realize our loss. The intensity of this loss is as instantly grasped as the effect of the crash itself. He stood for everything that was right, never for anything that was wrong."

MARY PICKFORD: "It is not the length of time we remain in this present human sphere that is important, it is what we do with that time. Will Rogers and Wiley Post gave gloriously of every moment, enriching our lives with the treasures of their accomplishments."

A SYMBOL OF AMERICA

Major Gen. JOHN F. O'RYAN: "Will Rogers dead! That is tough news for all of us. He was a symbol of America and Americans, yes, and of our institutions and the opportunities they hold for the ordinary young man of the country, if he will only combine with his ability the qualities of frankness and tolerance and real devotion to his country."

SIDNEY R. KENT, president of Fox Film Corporation: "All of Will Rogers' friends and co-workers in the Fox Film Corporation are inexpressibly shocked by this terrible thing. As big as this loss is to the Fox company, however, we must stand aside in recognition of the greater bereavement which has been visited upon his wife and family and indeed, upon all America. Will Rogers brought happiness and the cleansing influence of his good humor to millions and no eulogy from us could express the loss his death means to them."

GENE BUCK, President of the American Society of Composers, Authors and Publishers: "I can hardly believe that Will Rogers' voice is stilled forever. I do not believe we will see his like again."

IRVIN S. COBB: "He was a friend to all the world. Men like him, I'm sure, don't come along oftener than once in a century."

CONRAD NAGEL, the movie star, chose a selection from Shakespeare as the most fitting epitaph for his friend. It reads:

"His life was gentle, and the elements
So mix'd in him that Nature might stand up
And say to all the world, 'This was a man!'"